THE
CRYSTAL WISDOM
BOOK

THE CRYSTAL WISDOM BOOK

Cast the crystals for healing, insight and divination

STEPHANIE HARRISON
AND
BARBARA KLEINER

JOURNEY EDITIONS
BOSTON • TOKYO

PLEASE NOTE

Crystals can have a profound and far-reaching effect on your life. The adoption and application of the material offered in *The Crystal Wisdom Kit* is at the reader's discretion and sole responsibility. The authors, packagers and publisher of this book are not responsible in any manner whatsoever for any injury that may occur indirectly or directly from the use of this material. Crystals are not a substitute for normal personal healthcare and prompt medical attention where necessary. If you suffer from any health problems or special conditions please consult your doctor.

First published in 1997 by Journey Editions, an imprint of Tuttle Publishing, with editorial offices at 153 Milk Street, Boston, Massachusetts 02109.

Library of Congress Cataloging-in-Publication Data

Harrison, Stephanie, 1954–
   The crystal wisdom kit / by Stephanie Harrison and Barbara Kleiner.
      p.   cm.
   Includes bibliographical references.
   ISBN 1-885203-49-7
   1. Crystals—Miscellanea.   2. Crystals—Psychic aspects.   3. Precious stones—Miscellanea.
4. Divination.   I. Kleiner, Barbara, 1955–   .   II. Title.
BF1442.C78H37   1997
133`.2548—dc21   97–16728
                                                                  CIP

Distributed by

Charles E. Tuttle Co., Inc.	Tuttle Shokai Ltd.
RR1 Box 231-5	1-21-13, Seki
North Clarendon,	Tama-ku, Kawasaki-shi 214
VT 05759	Japan
Tel: (800) 526-2778	Tel: (044) 833-0225
Fax: (800) FAX-TUTL	Fax: (044) 822-0413

First Edition

05 04 03 02 01 00 99 98 97   1 3 5 7 9 10 8 6 4 2

AN EDDISON•SADD EDITION
Edited, designed and produced by
Eddison Sadd Editions Limited
St Chad's House, 148 King's Cross Road
London WC1X 9DH

Phototypeset in Truesdell and ZapfHumanist BT using QuarkXPress on Apple Macintosh.
Origination by C. H. Colour Scan, Kuala Lumpur, Malaysia.
Made and printed in China through Leo Marketing, UK.

CONTENTS

DEDICATION

May all the crystals, symbols and words contained within Crystal Wisdom
be dedicated so that they may only work for Highest Good in the name of love
and light. May each being who is inspired to work with Crystal Wisdom find
their own truth and wisdom and feel the blessings and guidance of the
Angelic who have overseen its creation.

WELCOME TO CRYSTAL WISDOM

'*The Crystal Wisdom Kit* has evolved as an inspirational tool which guides you into the enchanting world of crystals. It is our hope that by connecting with the crystals, you will be introduced to a new dimension which will awaken latent intuitional gifts and give you a fresh perspective in your life.

Each individual will resonate differently with the crystals and symbols – we feel it is important that you find your own truth and work in the way that feels right to you. Crystal Wisdom is only a guide to help you reach that point.

You will see many references to the "Light" contained within *The Crystal Wisdom Kit*. This refers to the energy which has many names, some might call it "God" and others the "Universal Life Force" or "Divine Wisdom". Please replace our words with those that have truth and meaning for you.

Our aim when we created Crystal Wisdom was to give a system of healing, divination and gaining insight, using the ancient magical qualities of crystals and symbols against a backdrop of astrological wisdom. We wanted it to be a fun and easy-to-use method, which can be operated at many different levels of consciousness, no matter what your experience.

Crystal Wisdom encourages you to explore the spiritual dimension and develop your connection with this part of the Universe. To ensure that you work safely and effectively we have included step-by-step instructions at the beginning of each relevant chapter. We have also included a chapter about vibrational healing with crystals – it is our hope that this will encourage you to want to learn more about this fascinating subject and explore your own truth and wisdom.

We wish you great joy, love and light as you take this journey of discovery into the world of crystals.'

Stephanie Harrison

Barbara Kleiner

How to use Crystal Wisdom: an Overview

Crystal Wisdom is an exciting and innovative concept which incorporates crystals, astrology and powerful symbols to give a unique system for gaining insight, divination and healing.

CONTENTS OF *THE CRYSTAL WISDOM KIT*

TWELVE HIGH-QUALITY CRYSTAL TUMBLESTONES FOR CASTING

CRYSTAL	APPEARANCE	KEYWORD
Amethyst	pale lilac to mid and deep purple	Transformation
Aventurine	pale to mid green with sparkly flecks	Expansion
Blue Lace Agate	pale blue with lace-like layers	Harmonization
Citrine	delicate golden yellow to deep brownish orange	Inspiration
Clear Quartz	totally clear and translucent	Clarification
Gold Tiger Eye	shimmering, banded brown and gold	Protection
Hematite	metallic black with silvery sheen	Preordination
Red Jasper	reddish brown	Manifestation
Rose Quartz	pale pink	Reconciliation
Snowflake Obsidian	jet black with white splashes	Illumination
Snow Quartz	opaque pure white	Purification
Unakite	pale green and orangey pink	Unification

THE LIFE WHEEL
Printed purple on white, the Life Wheel is divided into twelve 'life areas'. Each corresponds to a different aspect of life and contains symbols highlighting different facets of that area.

THE HEALING WHEEL
Printed gold on white, the Healing Wheel is made up of nineteen healing spheres, each one representing an aspect of your energy field – seven chakras, six realms of consciousness, five elements and 'All That Is'.

THE INSIGHT WHEEL
Printed white on blue, the Insight Wheel offers clear and simple guidance. It comprises nineteen spheres offering messages such as 'Go for it' or 'Hold back'.

BOOK AND POUCH
This illustrated book includes step-by-step instructions to using *The Crystal Wisdom Kit,* as well as sample readings and detailed guidance on interpretation.

A drawstring pouch is included to keep your crystals safe and for use when selecting crystals.

FAMILIARIZE YOURSELF WITH *THE CRYSTAL WISDOM KIT*

Identify your twelve crystal tumblestones by referring to the back of the box and the descriptions in the chart on page 7. If you want to know more about a particular crystal immediately, look up the relevant page in Chapter One. Now ascertain from the information on the previous page which wheel is which.

You may like to practise 'casting' the crystals. This means finding an effective way of dropping the crystals onto the wheels, ensuring that they fall randomly but that the majority land on the wheel. Try not to throw them too hard or from too great a distance. Select four or five crystals and find a way of casting them that suits you. Most people like to take the crystals and very gently rub them together between their palms,

as if rubbing their hands together. They then hold their hands, with the crystals pressed between the palms, some 5–8 centimetres (2–3 inches) above the centre of the wheel and let them drop. Others prefer to hold them in one hand and let them 'trickle' onto the wheel.

Now practise choosing crystals. Put the crystals into the pouch and, with your eyes closed, think to yourself 'May I attract the crystal which has a relevant message for me at this time,' and draw one crystal out of the pouch. First identify it, then look at the keyword from the chart or find the relevant page in Chapter One (*see pages 14–25*) and read more about the crystal you have chosen. Also turn to pages 12–13 to find out how to cleanse and dedicate your crystals.

HOW TO USE CRYSTAL WISDOM

You can use each one of the three wheels on its own or as part of a whole progressive reading.

The Life Wheel helps you to understand the current and future trends which surround you. Select five crystals from the pouch and cast these onto the wheel. They will fall into certain segments (known as life areas) and may land on particular symbols. By referring to the life areas indicated by the positions of the crystals (*pages 32–55*), you will find an explanation of the symbols and sample interpretations for each crystal on that life area. You can also refer to the crystal profile in Chapter One (*pages 14–25*) for more information about the crystals chosen and further suggested interpretations. For detailed step-by-step instructions see Chapter Two.

The Insight Wheel is a quick and simple way of gaining insight relating to a specific issue or question. It is especially useful when you require practical wisdom and guidance. It can be used

on its own for instant insight or as a progression from the Life Wheel for further clarification on an issue raised. Up to three crystals are cast onto this wheel, each giving a self-explanatory insight message. The aim is to give insight and guidance, not yes or no answers. For full instructions see Chapter Three, pages 59–63.

The Healing Wheel offers a simple but profound method of crystal healing. This can be used on its own as a healing tool or combined with a Life Wheel reading. The Healing Wheel is a reference map of the human energy system – each one of the nineteen spheres relates to a specific aspect of your energy field. Discover which part of your energy system requires balancing and healing by casting crystals onto the wheel to see which spheres are aspected. The crystals selected will give further insight regarding the healing qualities needed. Please follow the guidelines for use given on pages 65–70.

CRYSTAL WISDOM – THE CONCEPT

THE CRYSTALS

Crystals have been used throughout history as tools for divination and healing. They have been revered and valued by numerous civilizations such as the Mayans and ancient Egyptians, and their use has even been recorded in the Iron Ages. They can activate, enhance and amplify all that they connect with, when used with conscious intent and knowledge. Each crystal is unique, carrying its own particular theme and frequency and each individual will respond differently to the crystal.

As the crystals are cast onto the wheels, the appropriate symbols or messages will be highlighted by the position in which the stones fall. As the energies of the crystal and symbol combine, your intuition and inner knowing is activated and your gifts of insight and perception will be enhanced and amplified.

THE SYMBOLS

Symbols are found everywhere in life. They are an effective and immediate way of communicating abstract concepts. They speak to our subconscious and can act as triggers, keys and alarms within our psyche. Some will have very personal significance to an individual whilst others have a more universal appeal. Symbols are not necessarily geometric or pictorial – a ritual or dance is a moving symbol. Acts, such as exchanging rings, can also be symbolic.

The Life Wheel is based upon ancient astrological wisdom – astrology is thought to be the first science studied in the history of humankind, dating back to before 3000 BC in Mesopotamia and ancient Egypt. The twelve life areas are inspired by the twelve astrological houses and a variety of symbols have been inscribed onto this astrological backdrop. Symbols for the twelve signs of the zodiac and ten planets have been assigned to the most appropriate life area, in accordance with astrological tradition. A rune for each of the life areas has also been included, carefully chosen to encapsulate the primary theme of the life area. The runes are based upon an ancient Scandinavian system of divination and communication which dates back to the Ice Age.

The symbols used in Crystal Wisdom have been drawn from both ancient traditions and modern sources. The Egyptian hieroglyph representing the papyrus plant in the Plant Realm sphere in the Healing Wheel dates back to 3000 BC. The *Caduceus* in the sixth life area in the Life Wheel is the universal emblem for healing – it dates back to before 2600 BC and has appeared in many cultures throughout this period and is still used today by the medical profession throughout the world. The everyday symbols for recycling and the world-famous interlinked rings insignia for the Olympic Games, both found in the eleventh life area of the Life Wheel, are contemporary motifs and universally recognized.

The Insight Wheel purposely echoes the pattern of the Healing Wheel with nineteen spheres, eighteen of which contain clear and specific messages. The central sphere contains a symbol which represents a facetted gemstone and is reminiscent of an opening flower – this is a traditional symbol for the chakras (see page 65) as they open to higher levels of consciousness.

To begin with, you may wish to use the keywords which are attributed to each crystal – suggested interpretations are also given. However, as you become familiar with the crystals and symbols you will rapidly develop your own words and meanings. This will lead you to interpret the significance of the crystals in relation to their positions on the wheels in a way that is appropriate and right for you.

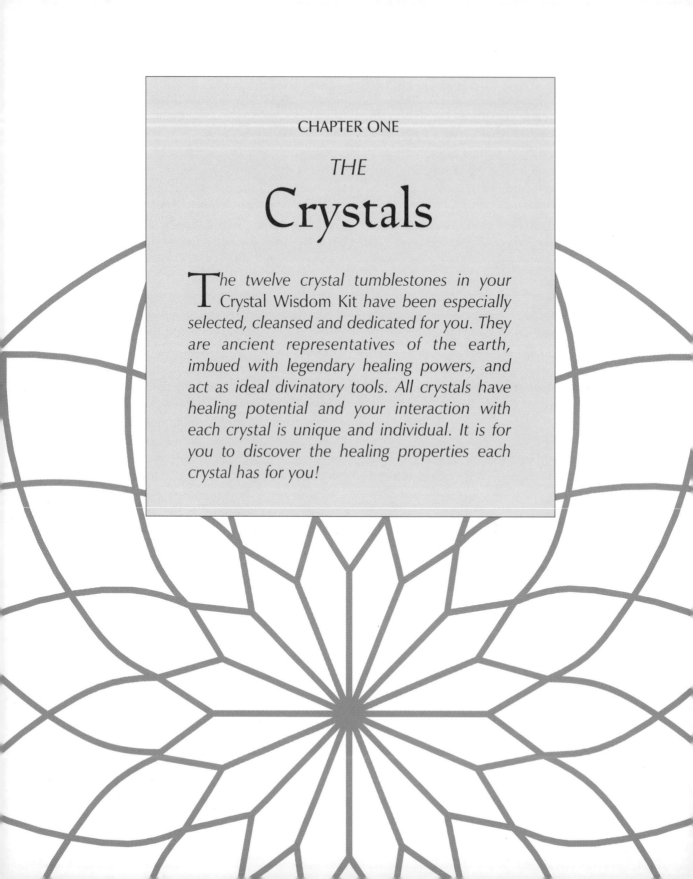

CHAPTER ONE

THE

Crystals

The twelve crystal tumblestones in your Crystal Wisdom Kit *have been especially selected, cleansed and dedicated for you. They are ancient representatives of the earth, imbued with legendary healing powers, and act as ideal divinatory tools. All crystals have healing potential and your interaction with each crystal is unique and individual. It is for you to discover the healing properties each crystal has for you!*

Introducing Crystals

Crystals are universally revered as objects of power and beauty. Crystals themselves are literally hundreds of millions of years old, 'born' from deep within the Earth herself. Some quartz crystals are estimated to be about 450 million years old and thought to have taken 200–300 thousand years to form.

Crystal is a word that is readily understood in many languages – it is a derivative of 'crystallos' which is Greek for 'ice'. The ancients used to think that, due to its glass-like appearance, quartz crystal was water which had frozen solid and called it 'frozen water from heaven' or 'solidified light'.

Every civilization is recorded as prizing crystals for their beauty, magical powers and healing qualities. Decorative or talismanic crystals and stones have been discovered in France that date back to 25,000 BC. Aristotle's successor, Theophrastus, wrote about the medicinal values of gems in the third century BC and Pliny's works of the first century greatly influenced medieval European thought on the healing properties of crystals. North American Indians carry medicine pouches and carve fetish animals out of indigenous stones. Bowls made of dark stone dating back to ancient times have been found globally – these were filled with water and used for 'scrying', the forerunner to gazing into a crystal ball. A polished granite sphere was found with some remains dating back to the Stone Age. Healing and divination with crystals is by no means a new phenomenon.

Legends have also evolved due to the use of crystals or because of their unique characteristics. The High Priest's Breastplate is referred to in detail in the Book of Exodus and tells of twelve precious stones decorating it. No one knows where the Breastplate is now and so it has become enveloped with mystery and intrigue.

WHAT IS A CRYSTAL?

Crystals are minerals which naturally form in the Earth and given the right environment can form into spectacular natural geometric shapes. The strict gemmological definition of a crystal is a mineral which has a regular atomic structure causing it to form in a regular geometric shape with flat faces. A quartz crystal forms naturally into a six-sided prism with a pointed termination made up of six triangular faces. Pyrite crystals are perfect cubes, whilst diamond crystals form into eight-sided octahedra shapes. Many people, unfamiliar with crystals, think that these have been carved.

'Crystal' is a term generally applied to all sorts of minerals, some of which, however, may not be crystals at all – for example, obsidian is a naturally occurring volcanic glass and has no regular atomic structure; it is therefore not possible for obsidian crystals to form.

Although usually referred to as 'crystal' healers, most therapists will also use non-crystalline minerals – typical examples are obsidian, amber and coral. These minerals have still formed within, or on the surface of, the Earth and are a part of the mineral realm. Although they do not have the internal regular atomic structure of a true crystal, they nonetheless share a resonance with their crystal counterparts and are equally respected and considered to have divinatory and healing properties.

ABOUT YOUR TUMBLESTONES

The twelve crystal tumblestones in your *Crystal Wisdom Kit* have been carefully chosen to encompass a wide range of healing frequencies and divinatory qualities *(see pages 14–25)*.

The stones display varying degrees of translucency from completely opaque to totally clear, a range of surface qualities – matt to metallic – and a whole spectrum of colours. All twelve are of similar hardness so, if carefully handled, will not damage each other when mixed in their pouch.

Each crystal is unique and your twelve tumblestones will reflect this. Look out for their distinguishing features – these may be clues to the special significance these crystals carry for you. Notice the variances in size and shape – some stones will be oval, others more oblong or square – you may find some remind you of a heart or pyramid. General descriptions are given on page 7, but each of your tumblestones will have its own pattern and colour. It may also have interesting designs or etch marks on the surface. Sometimes a crystal will contain within it other minerals or particles of matter; these are referred to as 'inclusions' and create distinctive patterns.

THE POWERS OF CRYSTALS

Crystals are examples of physical matter arranged in perfect symmetry, due to the regular internal and external structures. They are therefore considered to be 'patterns of perfection' which inspire balance and total alignment in surrounding energy fields.

They are also inspirational – in the same way that a beautiful landscape or moving piece of music can raise the spirits and open one's heart, gazing upon the natural beauty of crystals can open the consciousness to a wider perspective.

Some healers feel that the colour of a crystal explains its healing and divinatory properties and may correspond it with the traditional chakra colours. For example rose quartz or green aventurine may be considered 'heart chakra' stones and therefore to have soft, gentle and loving qualities.

Others feel that the mineral content gives the crystal its ability to heal, so hematite with its high iron content is considered good for the blood and the clay particles within red jasper can help to 'ground' a patient. Healing qualities of crystals are explored further in Chapter Five.

CLEANSING YOUR CRYSTALS

WHY IS CLEANSING IMPORTANT?

Crystals are extremely sensitive to thought, absorbing images and vibrations from those who handle them. So, cleanse your crystals regularly, especially if using them to give readings and healings to others. The cleaner your crystals, the clearer and more focused your readings and healings will be.

As you cleanse your crystals you will interact with them and strengthen your connection, facilitating a clearer link when you use them.

It is especially important to cleanse your crystals *before* and *after* using them with the Healing Wheel. Healing is a sacred act and it is a great privilege to be a part of this process. As the healer, it is your responsibility to ensure that the crystals are as pure as possible, so that they will transmit the clearest of healing frequencies for the benefit of the patient.

HOW TO CLEANSE YOUR CRYSTALS

A simple way to cleanse your crystals is to wash them in cool water. Hold them under a running tap or soak them for a few hours in still mineral water. Try adding a sprinkling of salt to the water – it is traditionally considered to have purifying qualities. All the crystals in your kit will happily respond to these watery cleansing methods.

You may like to try 'smudging' your crystals to cleanse them. To do this, hold them in your hand – one at a time or all together – and pass them through the smoke of some burning herbs, such as sage and lemongrass, or the smoke of an incense stick.

Some healers prefer to use visualization. They imagine the crystal is cleansed by holding an image in their mind and transmitting this into the crystals. See page 104 for further information on how to use visualization. Others like to leave their crystals in sunlight or moonlight for a few hours as they feel the light purifies the crystals.

All these methods work equally well. There may be times when you feel one method is more appropriate than the others – follow this feeling. Whenever working with crystals, it is important that you clearly focus your thoughts. Always try to hold the intention in your mind that the crystals will be cleansed as you hold them in the water, place them in sunlight or pass them through the smoke of an incense stick.

DEDICATING YOUR CRYSTALS

WHAT IS DEDICATING A CRYSTAL?

Dedicating your crystals ensures they can only be used in a positive way for good. In other words, they safeguard you and anyone who uses your crystals for readings and healings.

Crystals that have been dedicated cannot inadvertently pick up negative vibrations. So they may not need such rigorous cleansing – however, it is still a good idea to get used to regularly cleansing your crystals.

Dedicate your crystals when you first acquire your *Crystal Wisdom Kit*. It is not usually necessary to dedicate them each time you start a reading or healing, but some healers find this a helpful part of their preparation. You may, however, find you need to re-dedicate your crystals after periods of great change in your life, or if you have not used your crystals for a while. Dedicating is a useful way of familiarizing yourself with your crystals. It is also thought that each time you dedicate a crystal you also dedicate a part of yourself!

HOW TO DEDICATE YOUR CRYSTALS

To dedicate your crystals, hold them in one or both hands and either speak out loud or silently think the following:

'From this point on, may these crystals only be used in the name of love and light, always for Highest Good and Universal Purpose.'

Use words that have meaning and are true for you. Make sure you are totally sincere and focused when you carry out this dedication.

> Important Note: *The crystals in your kit have been cleansed and dedicated before reaching you. This is a safeguard in case people use them without first reading these instructions. However, it is far preferable for you to carry out the cleansing and dedicating process yourself – this will make these crystals truly yours, as your vibrations will meld and a link will begin to form between you.*

Amethyst

Amethyst ranges in colour from pale lilac to deep purple and is usually semi-translucent. It is often associated with meditation and changes in consciousness, carrying uplifting, transmutative qualities. Connect with the Amethyst frequency to increase spiritual awareness and change your life at many different levels.

Amethyst comes from the Greek word 'amethystos' which means 'not drunken'. In ancient times it was believed that the crystal could prevent people getting drunk – hence wine goblets were made out of Amethyst! It also has religious significance, being considered a stone of eminence, and features as one of the twelve crystals on the High Priest's Breastplate in the Book of Exodus. Its legendary protective qualities were called upon by Egyptian warriors, who carried Amethyst scarabs into war, and Native Americans who wore Amethyst to ensure they were not struck by lightning. Amethyst is a Quartz and is usually found in 'beds' of small points on a matrix rock, or alternatively as single crystals, pieces and smooth tumblestones.

Amethyst is often associated with the Crown and Brow Chakras, signifying a connection to a higher spiritual source. The colour purple is frequently linked to these chakras, which may explain why Amethyst is traditionally considered a high vibrationary crystal. Amethyst may help give you greater awareness of the soul impulse which guides you along your destined path. It encourages you to make time for contemplation and meditation. Working with this crystal may increase your sensitivity to subtle energies and give you greater awareness of the Divine influences surrounding you. Its effect may be difficult to quantify but, nonetheless, can be felt on many different levels. Some say this is an extremely 'spiritual stone' and others feel it helps you to remain on Earth and be comfortable in a physical body. It has many wide-ranging possible interpretations – the most important one is the one you feel most comfortable with.

Possible Divinatory Interpretations

A shift in consciousness is taking place within you, causing you to revise your whole outlook. Life changes may manifest, such as a change in residence or job. Qualities of spiritual upliftment and inspiration surround you – even everyday events hold special significance for you. Connect with the angelic aspects of the world – introduce the Divine into your mundane life. Prayer and meditation will help you make the transitions that occur at this time. Let go of old and redundant thought patterns.

All crystals have healing potential – your interaction with each crystal is unique and individual – discover the healing properties Amethyst has for you.

Aventurine

Aventurine is pale to mid green with sparkly flecks and is usually semi-translucent. Calming and soothing qualities are often linked to this crystal, which has associations with healing and nature. Connect with the Aventurine frequency to open your heart and mind to the spiritual frequencies within the Universe.

The name Aventurine was derived from the Italian 'a ventura', meaning a mistake. In the eighteenth century, a speckled form of man-made glass was discovered by accident in Venice, and Aventurine was named after this glass as it has a similar appearance. Sometimes it is mistakenly called 'Indian Jade'; this is definitely a misnomer as Aventurine bears no resemblance to Jade except for its colour. It is, in fact, a Quartz containing inclusions of tiny flakes of chrome fushcite mica, which account for the sparkly effect and the green colour. It is usually mined in compact rock-like formations and sold as rough chunks, polished pieces and tumblestones – single crystals are not found.

The gentle, soft-green colour combined with sparkly light-filled flecks may remind you to draw upon the healing powers of Nature. This could be as simple as walking in the park or feeling the grass beneath your feet; alternatively, you might consider looking at herbal or flower remedies. Aventurine is often associated with the heart and many healers feel it is a crystal which can help to balance and heal heartache and sorrow. It can encourage an expansion of the heart and a willingness to listen with the heart as well as the mind. It may also indicate an inherent ability to heal others and could be a sign of encouragement to develop your healing gifts. Aventurine can impart the courage required to explore the wider realms of the spiritual universe and may give you a feeling of safety whilst navigating uncharted territory in your spiritual journey. Befriend the Aventurine vibration and discover the unique way it can help you to expand your awareness.

Possible Divinatory Interpretations

Your life is moving into a phase of growth and expansion. Broaden your vision and look at the wider picture to see how you can grow as a person. Aspire to the highest at all times and avoid anything that limits you. Discover ways of increasing your knowledge and expanding your mind. This may be the time for you to develop your gifts as a healer. Find ways to set yourself free from old thought patterns and let the 'new you' emerge.

All crystals have healing potential – your interaction with each crystal is unique and individual – discover the healing properties Aventurine has for you.

Blue Lace Agate

Blue Lace Agate is a pale blue semi-translucent stone, interspersed with layers of milky-white Quartz giving a lace-like effect. This crystal is considered by many to be a traditional healing stone which has the ability to balance, integrate, calm and soothe. Connect with Blue Lace Agate to enhance your creative abilities, communicate more effectively and bring harmony into your life.

The name 'agate' originates from the river Achates in Sicily. The blue colour and 'lace' effect of the crystal accounts for its name. This blue is thought to be caused by iron pigmentation, and the white bands by inclusions of air bubbles, as in Milky Quartz. It usually occurs in banded chunks but occasionally groups of tiny crystals are found. Blue Lace Agate has been found suitable for engraving and it was used to make cameos in the fifteenth century. These were popular with the Germans, who became leaders in the Agate trade up to the nineteenth century – Ida Oberstein is still today one of the world centres for top-quality stone carvings. The Romans also prized engraved Agates of all kinds, including the blue lace variety. In ancient times, Blue Lace Agate was used as a talisman against idiocy and depression.

As a traditional healing stone, Blue Lace Agate has many different applications and is often used for general well-being in a crystal healing layout. It is often connected with the Throat Chakra and associated with aiding expression and creative ability, possibly facilitating pursuits such as singing, painting or writing. It can also be helpful in situations where it is especially important that you speak your truth. With the help of Blue Lace Agate, you may find you are able to access many different levels of understanding and wisdom. If you feel in need of a calming and balancing influence, try holding this crystal. When you need to communicate to a wide range of people, again enlist its help. With its layering and blend of blue and white, find out how Blue Lace Agate can help you work in more than one dimension at a time.

Possible Divinatory Interpretations

An aspect of your life may need healing at this time. Look below the surface and see the different factors at work and try to introduce a more harmonious atmosphere. Listen with your whole being and try to hear the truth behind the words. This may be a good time for you to explore and develop your gifts of healing, making your own healing process a priority in your life. Search for a way to balance and soothe a difficult situation. Ensure you speak your truth.

*All crystals have healing potential – your interaction with each crystal is unique and individual – discover the healing properties **Blue Lace Agate** has for you.*

Citrine

Citrine ranges in colour from pale yellow to golden orange and is usually translucent or semi-translucent. This crystal is associated with wisdom and spiritual upliftment, as well as more mundane qualities such as material gain. Connect with the Citrine frequency to feel joy and a sense of purpose as you get in touch with Divine Inspiration.

Citrine is named after 'citron' because of its lemony yellow colour; it is sometimes erroneously known as 'Spanish topaz'. It is part of the Quartz family, and it is thought that the colour is caused by iron contained within the structure; this usually occurs as purple coloured Quartz which is known as Amethyst, but when this is heated in the Earth the colour will change to yellow. Most commercially available Citrine is in fact Amethyst which has been artificially heated; natural crystals are relatively rare and expensive, the paler more yellow coloured stones being the most highly prized. Citrine is found as single crystals, beds of small crystals, known as 'druse', and as rough pieces. It was used as a talisman against the plague epidemic and was considered to be a gemstone in Greece in the Hellenistic period (336–27 BC).

Possibly due to its varying colours and degrees of translucency, Citrine is traditionally associated with many different healing qualities. In ancient times it was thought to protect against infection and have antiseptic properties. It also has associations with gold and riches and can help to bring wealth and abundance into your life. Connected with the Crown Chakra as well as the Solar Plexus and Sacral Chakras, some use Citrine to channel the cosmic wisdom. Other qualities often attributed to it are abundance, enthusiasm and limitless energy. It has a warmth and fire which makes it very popular as a gemstone as well as a healing crystal; some people find it makes them feel happy and enriched. Let the light-filled golden rays of Citrine help you make your connection to the celestial wisdom to discover what healing qualities it holds for you.

Possible Divinatory Interpretations

When Citrine comes into your life you are put on notice to be receptive to celestial wisdom: listen closely to your intuition and allow yourself to become inspired. Follow your instincts and do not ignore unusual ideas. Take up pursuits or study subjects which lift your spirits; and know that your words and actions can inspire others. As you allow yourself to be guided by your inner knowing, set your imagination free and remove all limitations. Know that you can do anything you set your heart on.

All crystals have healing potential – your interaction with each crystal is unique and individual – discover the healing properties Citrine has for you.

Clear Quartz

Clear Quartz is a translucent stone renowned for its clarity. It is considered to have powerful energizing and healing properties and is often regarded as the ultimate and universal healing crystal. It is frequently associated with amplifying, enlightening, cleansing and activating. Connect with Clear Quartz when you need clarification, energizing or focus.

The word Quartz comes from old saxon 'quertz' meaning cross vein ore. Myths and legends have always surrounded Quartz crystal. The ancients sometimes referred to it as 'frozen water from heaven' due to its glass-like appearance; it was also known as 'solidified light'. In Egyptian times, seals were made from it as were everyday objects such as bowls and vases, and, more unusually, crystal skulls and spheres. Both these latter objects were used for divination and worship as part of sacred rituals. Native Americans, Greeks and Romans are all recorded as using crystals for divination. The fascination still remains today. Clear Quartz, or Rock Crystal, as it is also known, is found as well-formed crystals, clusters and huge boulders as well as unusual formations, such as elestials, phantoms and double-terminated crystals.

Each individual needs to find out how they resonate with the Quartz frequency. For many, it will energize, activate and transmit. Others find it balancing, clearing and cleansing. Some healers feel it allows the flow of energy to move more freely. It is incredibly versatile and most crystal healers will include at least one single Quartz crystal in their healing kit. Many use it for directing energy – to strengthen the link to the Earth or to the Heavens. This energy can be directed towards parts of the energy system to disperse and clear blockages. Hold your Clear Quartz to draw from its strength and support, or place it on a part of the body that needs cooling or soothing. It can be a touchstone giving comfort in times of need and a point of focus when issues become clouded. Explore for yourself the universal healing properties of Clear Quartz.

Possible Divinatory Interpretations

You need to clarify certain issues within your life at this time, so you can clearly see your way forward. Explore ways of bringing some structure into your life and clarity into your thought processes. You may feel a need to clarify your part in the universal plan of life and discover its significance. Ensure your physical, mental and emotional states are balanced and focused, and clear away old lifestyle patterns, emotional debris and anything that is currently holding you back.

*All crystals have healing potential – your interaction with each crystal is unique and individual – discover the healing properties **Clear Quartz** has for you.*

Gold Tiger Eye

Gold Tiger Eye has distinctive bands of brown and golden yellow which combine to create a shimmering 'cat's eye' effect. This crystal is often associated with qualities of strength and grounding as well as material matters, and it is considered by many to be a stone of protection. Connect with Gold Tiger Eye when you need support, protection or earthing.

Gold Tiger Eye is aptly named due to its cat's-eye appearance, or 'chatoyancy'. It is a member of the Quartz family and contains inclusions of the mineral crocidolite, which give a fibrous effect, causing light to interact with the stone to give the characteristic shimmering appearance. Tiger Eye is most often seen in chunks or polished pieces – to fully appreciate its chatoyancy it needs to have a polished surface. For jewellery, it is commonly cut into a 'cabochon', an oval or circular dome which perfectly shows off the cat's-eye effect. Years ago, Tiger Eye was highly prized in Europe and cabochons were often seen in rings and brooches. It is a very popular stone with healers and crystal collectors alike – it has warm and vibrant colours and a light effect which is very attractive.

Traditionally Gold Tiger Eye is considered to have protective properties, usually in the sense of guarding possessions and people from worldly threats and dangers. It is also often called upon for earthing because it can be associated with mundane material matters. It may help you get in touch with practical issues, even manifesting prosperity. Consider its banded structure and layered effect which may help you to see what lies below the surface, encouraging you to look beyond the obvious and see what is really happening within a situation. It has a certain clarity and feels strong and positive so it might help you to be more forthright and feel your own potential for strength. You may find this a very invigorating crystal which energizes you and helps you to face challenges in day-to-day life. Get to know your Gold Tiger Eye and discover how it may become an ally in your life.

Possible Divinatory Interpretations

All is not as it seems on the surface at the moment. Exercise a little caution and look beyond the obvious – do not take everything at face value. Ensure you conserve your energies and make time to rest. Listen carefully to what is being said and think before you speak out. You may need to watch out for someone close to you. Take reasonable precautions to protect your property, your home and your values. There may be opportunities for wealth coming your way. Keep your feet firmly on the ground.

*All crystals have healing potential – your interaction with each crystal is unique and individual – discover the healing properties **Gold Tiger Eye** has for you.*

Hematite

Hematite has a shiny, black surface with a silvery, metallic sheen; it is completely opaque and is heavier than most tumblestones. It can be associated with fate and predestined events, and is often considered to have earthing, guiding and protective qualities. Connecting with Hematite may help you to anchor the light more effectively and fulfil your soul purpose.

Hematite comes from the Greek 'haema' meaning blood, due to the red colour seen on the surface of non-crystalline and unpolished stones. The characteristic metallic sheen occurs only on polished pieces, such as a tumblestone, and on natural crystal formations which have flat faces. The ancients believed Hematite could bleed because it turned water red when immersed in it, probably forming the belief that it could stem bleeding. Warriors carried it as they thought it made them invulnerable and indestructible, possibly explaining why it is often considered to be a 'cosmic shield'. Hematite consists mainly of iron, hence its density and hardness. It is usually found in both crystalline and rough form.

Traditionally Hematite is considered a 'grounding' crystal, which keeps you focused on earthly realities. Many healers also employ it for its protective qualities – the shiny silver surface is reminiscent of a mirror or shield which can reflect and deflect negativity. It is often associated with the Base and Sacral Chakras and physical healing situations. Another dimension to consider is its magnetic quality and its ability to carry a high light vibration in dense form. Some feel it can draw light to it, making it the ideal crystal to help anchor Divine Light into the earth plane. It is possible that Hematite can help you to recognize and play out your preordained role in the universal plan, helping you to see your fate, karma and destiny. Find out for yourself whether this crystal guides you inevitably to a predestined point on your soul path, or protects and grounds your energy field or works in another way that is unique to you.

Possible Divinatory Interpretations

Now is a time to look out for opportunities to explore your destiny and spiritual mission in this life. Draw strength from your past to help you live in the light in the present. Connections with others at this time may involve strong karmic links. You are reminded of the importance meeting the needs of your physical body as well as its spiritual counterpart. Remember the stronger your connection to the Earth, the more light you can connect to and hold. Ensure you stay aligned to the light at all times.

All crystals have healing potential – your interaction with each crystal is unique and individual – discover the healing properties Hematite has for you.

Red Jasper

Red Jasper is a deep terracotta colour and opaque. It is usually associated with grounding and practical qualities. It is a useful crystal to work with when dealing with earthly matters and when there is a need to discern what is real and what is illusory. Connect with Red Jasper to help your ideas and thoughts take form and to translate your inspiration into physical reality.

Red Jasper is part of the Quartz family and the earthy-red colour is appropriately caused by clay inclusions and iron oxide. The name Jasper is eastern in origin but of unknown significance, deriving from 'iaspis' (Greek), 'yash-pheh' (Hebrew) and 'yasb' (Arabic). Seals and amulets of Jasper have been found in various civilizations. It was used as an amulet against disturbances and drought as well as for protection from venomous creatures. Red Jasper was a popular stone used in mosaics. It is found in boulders and pieces but not as single crystals, and is usually sold as polished tumblestones or as rough hewn chunks of varying sizes.

Many healers use Red Jasper for its earthing qualities. They may give it to their patients to hold or place under their feet during a healing session to help keep them well anchored to the earthly realm. Its colour and constituents suggest that it is particularly well suited to this purpose – it is a vivid reminder of the Earth. One of the many benefits of being grounded is that energy will follow thought so ideas can manifest and become physical – this is the creative aspect to the application of Red Jasper. It can help to bring thoughts and ideas into being – essential for things to actually happen. The spiritual implication of this stone similarly lies in its ability to connect the energy field to the Earth. It is thought that the true task of every spiritual aspirant is to anchor the light vibration into the earth plane – to bring spirit into matter. Therefore every energy field needs to be earthed. Allow Red Jasper to help you play your part in bringing light into darkness and anchoring the spiritual vibration on Earth.

Possible Divinatory Interpretations

Turn your attention to practical matters and physical reality at this time. Make time to deal with earthly affairs. Constantly check to ensure that you are well grounded. It is possible now for ideas finally to come to fruition, so take action and make things happen. Keep your feet firmly planted on the ground; live absolutely in the present and celebrate being in your physical body, taking time to enjoy yourself on Earth. True spirituality is being able to anchor the light within the physical realm.

*All crystals have healing potential – your interaction with each crystal is unique and individual – discover the healing properties **Red Jasper** has for you.*

Rose Quartz

Rose Quartz is usually a pale pink colour and semi-translucent. It is often associated with soothing qualities such as forgiveness, comfort and softness, and it is most widely accepted in healing circles as the crystal representing unconditional love. Connecting to the Rose Quartz frequency may help to calm, whilst restoring peace and harmony.

Rose Quartz derives its name from its rose pink colour. It also occurs in a pale violet colour which is sometimes known as 'Lavender Quartz'. The colour is thought to be caused by manganese and possibly traces of titanium. Natural crystals are extremely rare – they have only been found in the last twenty to thirty years and are very small. It is usually seen as rounded, polished pieces such as tumblestones or as rough chunks of varying sizes. When cut into a sphere or cabochon, some Rose Quartz displays a star effect caused by inclusions of rutile needles. Today it is one of the most important and popular healing crystals. In spite of this – and that Rose Quartz beads dating back to 7000 BC have been found in Mesopotamia and it was used in jewellery by the Assyrians in 800–600 BC – very little is recorded historically about its uses.

The quality most often attributed to Rose Quartz is love – more specifically unconditional love. Perhaps this is the reason it has become one of the most widely used crystals for healing. Frequently it is the first crystal given to a patient. Its gentle qualities and soft colour make it very safe and accessible to all. It is usually associated with the Heart Chakra and issues of forgiveness and acceptance of oneself and others. Beyond these traditional applications, you may wish to consider a wider perspective, including its ability to help you love being of service on Earth – in this way Rose Quartz may be the crystal which helps you become comfortable in your physical body and more easily grounded. Its gentle delicacy can be deceiving; do not underestimate the power and limitless healing possibilities offered by the Rose Quartz frequency.

Possible Divinatory Interpretations

You are reminded that love is the greatest healer of all, and that self-healing can be your most important process. Find ways to forgive, love and appreciate yourself more. This may be the right time to bring about a reconciliation and introduce a greater degree of harmony and balance into your life. Remember to value your special gifts and talents. Allow yourself to surrender to the vibration of unconditional love – although this is not always an easy task.

*All crystals have healing potential – your interaction with each crystal is unique and individual – discover the healing properties **Rose Quartz** has for you.*

Snowflake Obsidian

Snowflake Obsidian is jet black and completely opaque with distinctive white 'splashes' resembling snowflakes. Qualities of clearing and guiding are often connected to this stone. It can represent the image of light shining at the end of a dark tunnel, giving a glimmer of hope after a challenging phase. Connect with Snowflake Obsidian to receive encouragement and motivation.

Snowflake Obsidian is distinguishable from the many other varieties of Obsidian by the white snowflake markings which give it its name. These markings are thought to be caused by the mineral chiastolite. The word Obsidian derives from 'Obsidius', which is a mistaken form of 'Obsius', the Roman who discovered Obsidian in Ethiopia. As it chips easily, it was originally used as arrowheads, knives and weapons in primitive times, while the Romans, Aztecs and Mayans used it for jewellery. It is not actually a crystal, but a volcanic glass which naturally forms under certain conditions when cooling takes place rapidly and there is insufficient time for the crystallization process to take place. The atomic structure of Obsidian is random and it is classified as 'amorphous'. Therefore, it does not exist as crystals; it is usually found as rough pieces.

Healers have varying thoughts about Obsidian: some feel it is grounding and others find it uplifting. The healing theme of Snowflake Obsidian is often one of bringing light into darkness and seeing the positive within the shadow, the silver lining of the proverbial cloud. It can help you to harness sufficient energy and motivation to break out of and through a difficult phase, and can give hope and encouragement that an end is in sight. Another perspective is to consider it as a stone which helps you transform by learning to recognize the potential within yourself. Pieces of Snowflake Obsidian vary tremendously – some are almost entirely black with just a hint of white while others are almost entirely white. This wide variance can explain the range of applications you may find for this stone. Hold it and see how you feel when you absorb its healing frequency.

Possible Divinatory Interpretations

A challenging and difficult time is coming to an end. You now have the ability to make a dramatic shift in consciousness so you can start to see life from a totally different viewpoint. As you feel yourself being guided along your path towards the light, experience enlightenment and spiritual inspiration. Try to see the good in other people and difficult situations. Allow yourself to be guided by your own spiritual truth and values.

All crystals have healing potential – your interaction with each crystal is unique and individual – discover the healing properties Snowflake Obsidian has for you.

Snow Quartz

Snow Quartz is an opaque, pure white crystal, frequently associated with purity, initiation and blessing. Healers find it has the ability to cleanse and rejuvenate the spirit as well as the physical body. Connect with Snow Quartz when you are seeking spiritual sustenance and gentle support.

Snow Quartz is named after its pure milky-white colour. The milkiness is caused by a large number of liquid inclusions, possibly carbon dioxide. It is usually found in rough hewn chunks rather than crystal points. Often considered a softer version of Clear Quartz, Snow Quartz has similar properties of cleansing and clearing without the highly active energizing aspect. However, it can have a powerful dimension that many underestimate.

Snow Quartz is a physical representation of pure white light – white light is made up of the seven rainbow colours combined in perfect balance and harmony. This stone therefore contains all the colours of the rainbow and could be considered to be a universal healing crystal for use almost anywhere in the subtle energy system. When white light is brought into the aura, the space is being cleared to allow a new higher vibration to enter. For a brief point in time the space seems empty, fears can surface and you may be called upon to clear old doubts and patterns of behaviour long forgotten. With the help of Snow Quartz, a clearing process unfolds making way for new, higher vibrations to enter the energy field, facilitating sudden and profound changes in consciousness. This powerful, life-changing experience could be described as an initiation. It is often associated with spiritual enlightenment and blessing, and, with its absolute purity, can help bring the whole energy system into alignment with the universal light frequency. Some healers consider it to be a symbol of a perfectly balanced energy field. Let Snow Quartz show you which light frequency you need to work with at this time.

Possible Divinatory Interpretations

Profound changes within the spiritual dimensions of your life are due to take place. Clear away old redundant behaviour patterns to make space for a new light-filled way of life. Before taking action, ensure your motives are pure. Look out for something in your life which needs cleansing and purifying. This may be an appropriate time to release yourself from past experiences and future expectations – simply live in the present. Whatever you are doing, ensure you work at the highest spiritual level you can.

All crystals have healing potential – your interaction with each crystal is unique and individual – discover the healing properties Snow Quartz has for you.

Unakite

Unakite, usually an opaque crystal, is a blend of pale green and salmon pink; sometimes one of these two colours will predominate. It is often associated with qualities of balancing, blending and harmonizing. Connect with the Unakite frequency to help unite seemingly irreconcilable energies.

Unakite is prized for its mottled colour and is very popular with amateur stone cutters as well as healers. Each piece will vary tremendously, ranging from predominantly green to predominantly pink. The green is due to the mineral Epidote, sometimes called 'pistacite' after its pistachio nut green colour. The salmon pink colour can vary from very pink through to very orange. These variations are accounted for by the fact that Unakite is actually a rock, not a crystal. It is made up of several minerals, namely Quartz, Pink Feldspar and Green Epidote. These are all commonly found individually, Feldspar and Quartz being two of the most common minerals on the planet. Unakite was originally found and identified in the Unakas range of mountains in North Carolina, USA, from where it derives its name.

Healers are attracted to the representation of duality which is symbolized by Unakite. They enjoy the blending of two different colours, showing different energies coming together in one harmonious whole. These factors can give insight into the healing qualities of Unakite. It is often associated with the Heart Chakra which is traditionally correlated with both green and pink colours, and Unakite ideally holds both frequencies in one. Both the green and pink colours are soft and have an earthy quality, which helps the healing to be grounded yet gentle and nurturing. If your healing work requires a theme of unity and duality you may usefully draw upon the qualities of this stone. To understand how you can anchor the spiritual vibration into the earth plane, harness the healing power of Unakite.

Possible Divinatory Interpretations

Your life may contain discordant strands of energy which need to be drawn together to make a cohesive whole. Find ways of marrying the active and passive parts of your being, discovering how you can create inner balance within yourself. Heal the past to move successfully on to the future. Look out for hidden meanings which may be present in messages received. Bring balance and harmony into your life. Look for compromise when resolving difficult situations. Aim to unite spirit and matter.

*All crystals have healing potential – your interaction with each crystal is unique and individual – discover the healing properties **Unakite** has for you.*

CHAPTER TWO

THE
Life Wheel

The Life Wheel allows you to gain insight into current and potential future trends which surround you, your friends and your family. At the same time, it helps you to develop your intuition in a simple but highly effective way. The wheel is divided into twelve equal segments, each representing an aspect of your life. These twelve segments, or life areas, are inspired by the astrological houses.

How to use the Life Wheel

The combination of crystalline energies together with ancient and modern symbols activates your inner wisdom and intuition, giving you enhanced gifts of insight and perception. Keywords are attributed to each of the twelve crystals and life areas; these are for guidance only – in time, as your understanding deepens, you will develop your own associations and themes for interpretation.

To familiarize yourself with the basic principles of the Life Wheel, start by giving yourself readings, following the step-by-step instructions below. Please pay particular attention to the preparation process – the clearer your focus and greater the degree of attunement, the more profound and effective your reading will be.

PREPARING TO GIVE A READING

It is a good idea to choose a quiet time for giving your reading. You may like to ensure that you are left undisturbed – unplug the telephone or switch on the answering machine, for example.

You will need:
- a comfortable chair
- a table (or other suitable flat surface)
- sufficient lighting to see the board clearly

Optional extras:
- a tape recorder or notepaper and pen (to make notes about the reading and stones you attract)
- a candle (to help you focus your intuition)

PREPARING YOURSELF
The greater degree of concentration and focus you can attain, the more effective the results and the deeper the insight will be. Listed below are four basic steps you need to take to ensure that you work safely and effectively with Crystal Wisdom. You may wish to light a candle before you begin this process.

1. **Relax your body:** take several long deep breaths concentrating on releasing any tensions in your body. Imagine that you are 'breathing out' the tensions through your feet.

2. **Ground your energies:** focus on where your body is connecting with the chair you are sitting on and make sure that your feet are flat on the floor. Imagine your whole body is getting heavier and that you are sinking deeper into the chair. See the section on earthing, pages 101–2, for further guidance on grounding your energy.

3. **Link to your source of inspiration:** imagine that you are now being surrounded by a bright and beautiful light which is flowing around and through you – make sure this light travels all the way through your body into your feet and into the earth beneath you.

4. **Ask for guidance and protection:** silently, using the words that feel right for you, ask:

'May I be guided and protected as I interpret these crystals and symbols to the best of my ability in a way that is right for my Highest Good at this time.'

Important Note: *You are advised to refer to pages 11–13 for information on how to work with crystals. This includes cleansing and dedicating crystals and ways of ensuring that you are working in the best and clearest way possible.*

READING THE LIFE WHEEL

1. Place all twelve crystals in their pouch and 'shuffle' them, either by shaking the bag gently or mixing them with your fingers.

2. Have a few moments of quiet and stillness – then ask, 'What influences are currently active in my life?'

3. Holding that question clearly in your mind, dip your hand into the pouch (left or right hand, whichever you prefer) and choose five crystals without looking. You can choose one at a time or in groups, whichever feels right for you.

4. Put the pouch with the remaining crystals to one side and now simply look at the five crystals that you have attracted to you at this time. Notice your initial reaction and immediate impression of these crystals. Are they very different and varying in colour and texture or are they mainly pale pastel colours or the deeper, stronger colours? How do you feel about your choice? Notice your reactions.

5. To identify which crystals you have chosen and their keywords refer to pages 14–25. The meanings of the crystals you have selected will become clearer as the reading progresses.

6. Now take your five crystals and very gently rub them together between your palms. Hold your hands, with your crystals pressed between

your palms, some 5–8 centimetres (2–3 inches) above the centre of the Life Wheel. Ask that you now be shown, 'How and where are these energies manifesting in my life at this time?' With that thought, continue to rub your hands together and gently let the crystals fall from your hands onto the wheel. You may find other ways of casting your crystals as you become more familiar with Crystal Wisdom. However, always keep the question clearly in mind as you both hold and cast the crystals.

7. Allow yourself a few moments just to look at the wheel as a whole and the patterns that the crystals may have formed. Do not rush to interpret anything at this stage; just let your eye be

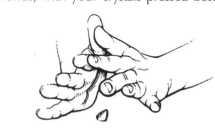

> Important Notes:
> • If a crystal has fallen outside of the wheel, you can either choose to disregard it or to draw it towards the centre of the wheel very slowly in a direct line until it is brought into one of the wheel's segments. However, make a mental note that this stone may have a much more distant and peripheral influence on the reading.
> • Sometimes the crystals fall so that one or more may bridge two segments. You may like to interpret this as both life areas being equally influenced – a suggested interpretation for combinations of life areas is included on the first page of each life area.
> • Occasionally, a crystal will fall absolutely in the centre of the chart. This could be interpreted as an over-riding influence being exerted in all areas of life, or the quality of the crystal in the centre might suggest a general theme which needs to be drawn into your life at this time.
>
> Please also refer to Hints for Interpreting the Life Wheel on page 30.

naturally drawn to certain key areas.

8. Each of the twelve segments represents an area of life – its name appears on the Life Wheel alongside different symbols representing more detailed aspects of the life area. Now start to connect each crystal to the life area in which it has fallen. Then look at its energetic significance and keyword and explore the possible meanings and associations of this. You may find it sufficient just to look at the keywords for the crystals and the symbols on the Life Wheel, and from that find you are able to develop your own picture and interpretation. Or you may prefer to read the sections relating to the specific life areas indicated in your reading (see pages 32–55). For each life area, the key issues it relates to and the questions it poses are discussed. The meanings of the symbols used on the Life Wheel are explained and the possible significance given. There is also a suggested interpretation of how to combine the issues of each life area with its neighbours, should a crystal bridge the two areas. In addition, the Life Challenge for that area is discussed. (For a specific Life Challenge reading, see Discovering Your Life Challenge, page 30). And, finally, a suggested interpretation is given for each of the twelve crystals within that area.

READING THE LIFE WHEEL

1. 'Shuffle' the crystals.
2. Ask, 'What influences are currently active in my life?'
3. Choose five crystals.
4. Examine the crystals you have chosen.
5. Identify the crystals and the keywords associated with them.
6. Ask, 'How and where are these energies manifesting in my life at this time?' and cast the crystals onto the wheel.
7. Contemplate the wheel and note the positions of the stones on it.
8. Connect each crystal's energy with the significance of the life area it has fallen on.
9. If appropriate, continue the reading using the Insight Wheel or Healing Wheel.

---

9. Your reading now becomes much more detailed – you may find that certain symbols within the segment will give you specific clues regarding the interpretation. Finally, you may wish to go on to seek some specific guidance via the Insight Wheel or to experience the healing qualities of crystals, in which case you could use the Healing Wheel.

COMPLETING A READING

Pick up all the crystals you have used for the reading and cleanse them (see pages 12–13) prior to placing them back in their pouch.

Make notes of the reading, including the stones you selected and keywords plus any other impressions or information that emerged. Remember to note down the date of the reading for reference. You may even wish to start a journal, so you can keep a record of your readings and see how your divination skills develop.

Put the wheels away. As you return them to the box, affirm that you are also 'closing down' your intuitive gifts at this time.

Stand up and have a good stretch, rub your hands together firmly in order to ensure you are well grounded.

Finally, blow out the candle if you used one.

For further information on closing down and clearing the higher subtle energies you have invoked, please see page 105.

READING FOR OTHERS WITH THE LIFE WHEEL

When you read for someone else follow the same procedure, except:

- Ensure you can read the board easily. You may wish to ask your 'client' (the recipient of the reading) to sit opposite you with the board and crystals between you.

- Ask your client to select the five crystals from the pouch, with their eyes closed, whilst focusing on the question, 'What influences are currently active in my life at this time?'

As you develop your intuition and confidence and read for more and more people, you may find that the emphasis and meanings of the crystals will change, depending on whom you are reading for. When you become more practised with this system, you may wish to expand the method and use some of the techniques described on the opposite page.

HINTS FOR INTERPRETING THE LIFE WHEEL

The aim of this section is to give you some guidance on how you can develop your skills as a 'crystal reader'.

- When you first start reading, you might find it helpful to read the section relating to each crystal you have selected, so you have various ideas as to how it might be interpreted. Then, immediately afterwards, read the section on the particular life area where the crystal has fallen, so you can see all the different types of life events, activities and areas that might be indicated by that segment. This section includes a sample reading for each of the twelve crystals.

- The order in which you read the crystals is personal to you, but quite often you will see that a particular crystal or life area catches your attention. Two or more crystals may fall in one part of the wheel – this is obviously a particularly important area of life for you at this time and could be a good starting point for the reading.

- You may find that out of the five crystals, there is one that continues to mystify you. It is often better to just 'let that go'. Make a note of the crystal, its keyword and the area where it fell and you may find, in the coming weeks, that its significance will become apparent to you. In this way you will develop your own meanings for the crystals and how to interpret them.

- Write your own set of keywords for the twelve crystals and the twelve life areas, expressing what the crystals and life areas mean to you.

- Keep a written note of all the readings you do, carefully noting the date. Then look back to see how accurate you were; in this way you can understand what message each crystal is conveying to you.

- Give lots of readings, especially for yourself, and in this way familiarize yourself with the crystals and what they mean to you.

- Remember the keyword is just that – the key to unlock your inner knowing!

DISCOVERING YOUR LIFE CHALLENGE

To give a more spiritual dimension to the reading, you may ask 'What Life Challenge am I working on at this time?' Then choose up to three crystals and cast these onto the wheel. For this reading, refer to the Life Challenge texts relating to the life areas indicated by the crystal placement. Note that three challenges is more than enough! Often only one crystal will fall within the wheel, or all three crystals will fall into a single life area, highlighting just one Life Challenge.

VARYING AND EXPANDING YOUR READING TECHNIQUES

So far, an outline for a very basic reading has been given. As you gain experience, you can develop your technique and make your readings far more complex. Some ideas for doing this are listed below.

● Instead of casting five crystals, select seven, so you end up with seven different influences to interpret. This gives a more in-depth reading, offering a broader perspective on the influences at work in life. Because the spread of crystals, themes and symbols will be more wide ranging, a greater level of expertise is required of the reader.

If you wish, although the method becomes even more complex, you can use all twelve crystals and interpret the twelve vibrations according to where they fall. In this type of reading you concentrate far more on the significance of the life areas being activated rather than what energies are coming to the client. The more crystals that are used, the greater skill required from the reader. Note that any number of crystals can be selected – as few as one, or all twelve – your own preference and style will develop in time.

● After the initial reading of five crystals, choose an extra one or two crystals from those remaining in the pouch in order to clarify or expand a particular aspect of the reading.

For example, if Clear Quartz (keyword: clarification) has fallen into the Partnerships life area, you may wish to know what type of partnerships this is referring to. To do this, you then choose one or two stones from the pouch, asking for clarification – then cast the one or two stones onto the wheel. If the stones fall into the 'career' segment, it is most likely a business partnership, but if the stones fall into the 'pleasure' segment, it is more likely to be a romantic relationship. If stones fall in each, then both types of relationship may be suggested. Also, the stones selected will give clues – if you have chosen Rose Quartz it is more likely to be an emotional aspect of partnerships than Red Jasper which has a more practical, earthy quality.

● Instead of asking about the 'influences currently active in your life', ask more specific questions. Note, however, that if a very specific question is being asked, it is sometimes useful to restrict the number of crystals chosen to only two or three – this makes it easier to keep the focus. A series of several questions can be asked.

For example, you may wish to ask, 'What energies do I need to draw into my life at this time?' Then, once the crystals have been chosen, ask, 'Where should I direct these energetic influences?' This gives a different emphasis and looks more at manifesting energies and consciously drawing them into your life. You can apply this to a particular area of your life which is currently troubling you.

● At the end of the reading, with your eyes closed, choose just one crystal from all those used for the reading to see which influence and area is of prime importance at this time. To do this, group them together on the wheel or in one hand and select one crystal with your eyes closed. Be especially aware of the message that crystal carried and which life area it fell into. You can also deepen and reiterate the message of this crystal and its placement as a useful way of giving a summation and completion to the reading session.

The Self

PERSONALITY

PERSONAL POWER

INDIVIDUALITY

SELF-REALIZATION

Butterfly

Lightning Flash

The first life area is all about you, your inner being, your inner child and the various levels of your own soul. You are guided to look within for answers. Crystals in this life area can indicate experiences which are 'preordained' to help you meet life lessons that are a part of your destiny. Opportunities for soul growth can be indicated in this life area.

Do you really know who you are and are you truly expressing your inner being? In what way are you being reborn at this time? What transformation processes are taking place within your life? How can you aid your spiritual development and levels of self-awareness?

Look out for crystals in the first life area to help you recognize and understand life events that are taking place to aid your process of self-discovery. These events could help you to find your place within the cosmos and fulfil your spiritual destiny. Ancient wisdom always advises 'know thyself' and that can be one of the hardest lessons of all.

THE SYMBOLS

Fiery and pioneering *Aries*, the first sign of the zodiac, and the dynamic planet *Mars* oversee the first life area, perfectly symbolizing initiation, birth and new beginnings. The *Butterfly*, Greek symbol of the soul, represents liberation and transformation in the metamorphosis of the caterpillar into the butterfly. The *Lightning Flash* demonstrates that spark of realization which takes place when, through inspiration and intuition, we suddenly understand an aspect of ourselves. The *Mystic Eye* encourages you to use the focused single eye of enlightenment to look within to give increased perception and inner vision. The *Twin-faced Head* asks you to look at yourself without the mask you usually don for the outside world – accept yourself as you truly are. The *Bridge* is a traditional symbol for crossing from one level of consciousness to another, whilst the river shows the continuity and connectedness of all things within the Universe. The rune *Jara* represents the perfection of will and a powerful personality.

Crystals spanning the twelfth and first life areas remind you to ensure the beliefs you express and portray to the world are truly your own and relevant to you at this time in your life. If the first and second life areas are indicated, examine the wealth within your inner being.

Mystic Eye

Twin-faced Head

Bridge

Aries

Mars

Jara

THE LIFE CHALLENGE

The first life area challenges you to experience and understand the meaning of 'isolation'. Learn how to become a distinct and unique individual without becoming solitary and setting yourself apart from others.

The way you hold the Divine vibration is unique and individual to you. The vibration contained within is universal. The challenge is to ensure the Light shines through you in a way that is a true representation of your soul essence.

CRYSTAL INTERPRETATIONS

Amethyst
A profound change is due to take place within you. Allow inner changes to take place peacefully and smoothly – try not to resist your transformation.

Aventurine
Let your whole being expand into the 'new you'. Do not let old fears or doubts limit you at this time.

Blue Lace Agate
Balance the needs of your inner being with the more extrovert aspects of your personality. Accept yourself for who and what you are.

Citrine
Let your soul essence shine through and allow yourself to become a point of inspiration for others around you. Listen to your intuition.

Clear Quartz
Get to know yourself better and be clear about who you are and where you want to be. Ensure the real you is projected and expressed.

Gold Tiger Eye
Conserve your energies and look after yourself – get plenty of rest. Do not allow others to invade your personal space or over-influence you.

Hematite
You are put on notice that your soul has a mission to fulfil in this lifetime! Make sure you are grounded.

Red Jasper
Make sure you are well grounded and dealing with practical issues in your life. Make time to deal with earthly affairs.

Rose Quartz
Do you need to love and appreciate yourself more? Value what you give others and spend more time and energy on pampering yourself.

Snowflake Obsidian
There is an opportunity for you to realize your own soul purpose at this time. A challenging and difficult phase is coming to an end.

Snow Quartz
Allow yourself to release the past and move into a new Light-filled way of living. Time to let go of redundant thought patterns.

Unakite
Seek to balance and harmonize seemingly conflicting aspects of your personality. Marry the active and the passive parts of your being.

Prosperity

Diamond   *Coin*

The second life area relates to material matters, personal values, your ability to appreciate your possessions and your potential for wealth. It shows your desires for that which makes you feel secure and stable and what you may hope to gain in this life. Seek guidance here regarding your potential for wealth and how to use your gifts and possessions positively.

Do you enjoy and share your wealth or is it a source of anxiety? Are you being true to yourself or have you inherited your values from family, friends or a partner? Have you lost sight of what is really important to you? Are you taking good care of yourself? Do the people around you appreciate your talents? Is it time to ask for a pay rise?

Look out for crystals landing in this life area if you wish to know more about money, material issues or what makes you feel stable and secure.

THE SYMBOLS

The practical and earthly zodiac sign of *Taurus* and planet of feminine harmony, *Venus*, aptly remind us of the need to be creative and manifest earthly goods whilst remaining in balance. The *Diamond*, most famous of all gems, is prized for its brilliance and seeming indestructibility. It symbolizes treasure and wealth and is an enduring symbol of the earth's fabulous resources. The *Coin* is a traditional representation of worldly goods and payment for debts due. It is inscribed

with the head of the ruler of the time, symbolizing material power and success. The *Scales* encourage you to weigh up the values by which you live. Egyptian mythology suggests that at the end of his life, a man's heart is weighed against a feather – perfectly balanced scales show a life lived with integrity and high spiritual values. The *Money Chest* safeguards your true values; it allows you to preserve something for future generations or may remind you to start saving now for the proverbial rainy day. The *Norse Money Charm*, an ancient symbol, suggests that you allow yourself to be open to receive that which is due to you. The rune *Daeg* symbolizes fruition, growth and prosperity, possibly in material circumstances.

Crystals bridging the first and second life areas suggest you examine the wealth within your inner being. If the second and third life areas are indicated then consider how your possessions have become an outward expression of yourself.

Scales

Money Chest

Norse Money Charm

Taurus

Venus

Daeg

THE LIFE CHALLENGE

The second life area introduces the test of ownership. Can you use, enjoy and then release your possessions and wealth to give your prosperity meaning? In this way, wealth is regenerated and continues in an abundant life cycle.

The only point in having possessions is if they help you to develop spiritually; holding on to what we own merely ensures a spiritual stagnation. Can you put your gifts and possessions to meaningful use now?

CRYSTAL INTERPRETATIONS

Amethyst
You may now experience a change in your financial circumstances. It is very likely that your whole value system will be re-evaluated.

Aventurine
Allow yourself to receive and build up your reserves of money or energy. Make sure you profit at many different levels during a period of plenty.

Blue Lace Agate
Accept your material needs and appreciate what you actually have. Balance your need to save for the future with having sufficient resources to live for today.

Citrine
Follow your instincts; this is the time to play your hunches with regard to money matters. Come up with some unusual ideas for making money.

Clear Quartz
Clarify your values – what do you hold to be truly dear and important in your life? Bring some structure into the material part of your life.

Gold Tiger Eye
This is a time to be careful with money, possessions and all that you hold dear. Guard your belongings well and be extra aware of security.

Hematite
Manifest your own values in your life; no longer adhere to other people's ideals. You are drawing to you that which you have earned in the past.

Red Jasper
There are excellent prospects for material wealth at this time. Possessions that you desire may be more easily obtainable now.

Rose Quartz
Allow yourself to be wealthy materially as well as spiritually. Take time to enjoy your belongings and possessions, remember you deserve them!

Snowflake Obsidian
See the benefit and 'profit' in what you first perceived to be a loss. Enlightening information is available for you to use to your advantage.

Snow Quartz
Clear out old possessions and belongings which may be holding you back. Ensure your values and ethics are totally pure.

Unakite
Reconcile your spiritual wealth with your material wealth. Trust you will receive what you need in life, rather than what you think you want.

Communication

CREATIVITY

INTELLECT

KNOWLEDGE

SHORT JOURNEYS

Work of Art

Open Book

The theme of the third life area is communication and creativity, encouraging you to look at how you express yourself. Matters concerning brothers, sisters and peer groups may show up here, as well as those of early education. Crystals cast into this life area ask us to look at issues such as how we express our needs.

Do you really speak your truth – are you totally able to express your inner being? Do you really communicate what you want, whether at work or at home? Is your life a true expression of your innermost needs?

If you want to know more about how you think and express yourself, look in this life area. Significant short journeys can also be indicated when crystals fall in this area.

THE SYMBOLS

Witty and versatile *Gemini*, the twins of the zodiac, and the planet *Mercury*, winged messenger of the gods, encapsulate the communicative and versatile theme of the third life area. The *Work of Art* shows creative communication; through art you can communicate your deepest feelings and emotions. The *Open Book* symbolizes ancient knowledge and wisdom, including that which is already known and that which is yet to be discovered. It also records your words, thoughts and deeds, leaving a legacy of your creative power to inspire others who follow you.

The *Key* sets you free to express your true power and discover reality beyond outward appearances. It symbolizes a special gift given as a well-earned reward. *Footprints* show you leaving your imprint on Earth as you travel through life, uniquely expressing yourself by the way you make your journey. The *Tree of Knowledge* is a traditional representation of the paths of communication between Heaven and Earth. Celestial wisdom is rooted in the physical plane – the entwined serpent shows the journey of self-creation and self-knowledge, whilst the fruit feeds the creative impulse. The rune *Ansur* is sometimes known as the 'messenger rune' and can indicate a journey to acquire information and knowledge.

If the second and third life areas are aspected consider how your possessions have become an outward expression of yourself. If the third and fourth life areas are indicated, look at what your family life says about you to the outside world.

Key

Footprints

Tree of Knowledge

Gemini

Mercury

Ansur

THE LIFE CHALLENGE

The third life area tests our ability to transmute intellect into spiritual intelligence. To live intelligently is to live responsibly. Energy follows thought. Can you take full responsibility for every one of your thoughts?

The power of seed thoughts must germinate into conscious light lived fully in daily life. Does your life fulfil the dictates of your soul being? Can you express the power of life and light via conscious thought in your daily life?

CRYSTAL INTERPRETATIONS

Amethyst
Proceed on your spiritual path taking small but certain steps forward. Even the shortest of journeys can bring their own rewards.

Aventurine
Increase your contact with friends, old and new. Studying, however informally, could turn the key and let your mind expand.

Blue Lace Agate
Start to learn how to utilize your knowledge wisely. Balance what you want to say with what others need to hear.

Citrine
It is time to express yourself with greater enthusiasm and clarity. You have the ability to inspire others when you communicate.

Clear Quartz
Express yourself with clarity and truth to avoid giving out mixed and muddled messages. Learn about something which really interests you.

Gold Tiger Eye
Be careful with how you use words, even in casual conversation or written notes. Allow extra time for short journeys; unexpected delays may occur.

Hematite
Energy follows thought – what you think becomes reality. This is the time for you to communicate your spiritual message to another.

Red Jasper
Friends and siblings may inspire you to take action on a project you have been thinking about. Consider writing or find some other creative outlet.

Rose Quartz
Choose your words carefully now, ensure they carry love and not malice. Opportunities for you to offer words of comfort to others may arise now.

Snowflake Obsidian
Words of inspiration and solace can comfort and support those who grieve. Communication occurs at many different levels, not just with words.

Snow Quartz
Speak your truth at all times whilst considering those who must listen to you. Express yourself with purity at every level of communication.

Unakite
Try to look equally at both sides of an argument. Look for the inner message within a situation as well as the obvious outer statement.

Home

ANCESTORS

FAMILY

EMOTIONS

SECURITY

Tree with Roots   *Heraldic Shield*

The fourth life area relates to your roots, family values, and inherited patterns of behaviour. It may also refer to your home life, including practical aspects, such as a possible house move or need to renovate your home. At a deeper level issues relating to your ancestral past and possibly even past lives may show up here. Your emotional security and safety in the world will be raised in this area.

Is your home life sufficiently supportive so that you may relax, rejuvenate and refresh your spirit there? Is a change of residence indicated? Is it time for you to heal the past in order to move into a new phase in the future?

Crystals in this area will ask you to look at your roots, your home life and family relationships. Deep-rooted needs for security and feeling safe can emerge here. You may wish to re-examine your role within your family. Aspects relating to your home will also show up here.

THE SYMBOLS

Sensitive and protective *Cancer* and the emotional, instinctive influence of the *Moon* help you to feel at a profound level and rediscover the roots of your intuition. The *Tree with Roots* represents both the different branches of your family tree and the importance of recognizing and maintaining your roots in order to create firm foundations. The *Heraldic Shield* shows the history, ancientness and continuity of the family, united under one banner, which is your family identity. The *Snail* reminds you that you can create a home wherever you place your heart and soul. Remember to guard this space by imagining a protective shell which surrounds you at all times, and is constantly renewed by your spiritual intent. The *Family Unit* symbolizes relationships with family members and the core of your support system. It can help you identify your place within the family hierarchy. The *Castle* represents the universal need for security, safety and a place of spiritual refuge. It reminds you to take sensible precautions to ensure that you have a home to retreat to which is also physically safe and secure. The rune *Peorth* is the hearth or centre of the abode which is the crucial point around which the family unit revolves.

If the third and fourth life areas are indicated, look at what your home and family life say about you to the outside world. The fourth and fifth life areas suggest you enjoy your home and make it an environment for pleasure and leisure.

Snail

Family Unit

Castle

Cancer

Moon

Peorth

THE LIFE CHALLENGE

The fourth life area challenges you to find the centre of your being. Seek the pivotal point around which your soul revolves. When you find your true centre, the foundation of your spiritual being can establish roots and so liberate the soul.

When you are truly centred, the soul is free to explore its path. You need strong stabilizing foundations to help you assimilate the lessons that life offers. How can you be more centred in order to follow your Divine path?

CRYSTAL INTERPRETATIONS

Amethyst
Do you wish to move house or at least change your home environment? Family members may be undergoing major shifts in their lives.

Aventurine
Look back on your past for possible enlightenment into who, why and what you are. Could this be the time to expand your space at home?

Blue Lace Agate
Heal past family quarrels to build a firm foundation for future happiness. Ensure your home environment is peaceful and tranquil for you at this time.

Citrine
Consult with family members for guidance and advice. Is it time to renovate your home, to create a space in which you feel inspired and secure?

Clear Quartz
Clarify where you really stand in relation to family issues. Do you need to distance yourself from family members or problems at home?

Gold Tiger Eye
Protect your property, home and family. This may be a good time to keep your distance from some family members.

Hematite
Make your home a temple for the Light. Draw strength from your past to help you live now in the Light.

Red Jasper
Deal with all family matters in a very practical and down-to-earth way. Home improvements could be placed on your agenda now.

Rose Quartz
It is important to maintain a home environment that is loving and soothing. With love and acceptance, reconciliations within family relationships may occur.

Snowflake Obsidian
A testing time within family relationships is now coming to an end. Conflict and disharmony may actually have cleared the air and resolved old issues.

Snow Quartz
Ensure your home environment is cleansed, both in the physical and spiritual sense. You may be due for a major rethink with regard to family issues.

Unakite
How can you bring balance and harmony to a family situation? Heal the past to move successfully on to the future.

Pleasure

ROMANCE

HOBBIES

CHILDREN

INSPIRATION

Linked Hearts

Musical Notes

The fifth life area relates to your inspirational spark and ability to be creative. It shows your capacity for play, having fun and following pleasurable pursuits and hobbies. Aspects relating to children will show up in this area, as will matters of the heart such as romantic interludes.

Are you making enough time in your life to play and have fun? Does your inner child need to be nurtured and allowed a greater degree of expression? When was the last time you felt inspired and passionate? How can you bring some zest and exuberance into your life?

Crystals in this area encourage you to remember or find out what you really enjoy doing and what makes you feel good. Through having fun you can bring your life back into harmony. You are also reminded of the importance of loving relationships both with partners and children.

THE SYMBOLS

Energetic and warm-hearted *Leo*, combined with the vibrant and powerful planet of the *Sun* suggests you enjoy life to the full. *Linked Hearts* traditionally symbolize romance and love affairs as well· as that unconditional affection felt for pets and close friends. This may be a time to open your heart to various romantic possibilities or allow yourself to unite with another. *Musical Notes* remind you to enjoy yourself with creative

pursuits, like listening to or playing music. Allow yourself time to discover latent talents and gifts through hobbies. The *Cradle* represents the children in your life and your inner child – reconnect with the innocence, freshness and spontaneity of childish behaviour. The *Maypole* indicates shared celebrations and joy. These are times of coming together to rejoice with traditional celebrations which are a part of the dance of life, such as a marriage or baptism – celebrate the creative life force. The *Spinning Top* encourages you to indulge in carefree play to recapture the exuberance of youth through movement to find your true inner core. The rune *Beorc* represents the birth of life, fertility and the mother–child relationship.

If crystals span the fourth and fifth life areas, you are reminded to enjoy your home and make it an environment for pleasure and leisure. The fifth and sixth areas suggest you try to find pleasure and joy whilst working in service to others.

Cradle

Maypole

Spinning Top

Leo

Sun

Beorc

THE LIFE CHALLENGE

Channel your creative life essence with absolute purity. Ensure you sound your true note within the life symphony. Do you know your truth and can you act out your part in the life drama with total purity?

Demonstrate, by the way you participate in life, that you can be a pure and clear agent for the release of the power and energy you carry. Are you expressing who and what you truly are? Are you a true expression of yourself?

CRYSTAL INTERPRETATIONS

Amethyst
It is time to meet your own needs and desires, not those imposed on you by others. Ensure your spare-time pursuits give you real pleasure.

Aventurine
Make more time to have fun and enjoy life. Children could be a source of great joy and healing for you at this time.

Blue Lace Agate
Allow yourself enough time for pleasure and play – choose pursuits which calm the mind and restore your body back to balance.

Citrine
Could you be due to meet someone very special, who will have a profound effect on your life? Express your dreams and desires.

Clear Quartz
Re-evaluate how you want to spend your free time and make sure you do what you enjoy most. Be clear about what you ask for.

Gold Tiger Eye
Exercise a little caution with hobbies and pursuits of pleasure. A romance may not be all it seems at this time – take care!

Hematite
Let the inspirational spark burn bright and deep within you. Allow your inner child the freedom to express its essence fully.

Red Jasper
Enjoy yourself more and participate in fun pursuits which appeal to you and have practical applications. Celebrate being in your physical body.

Rose Quartz
A time of giving and receiving love, even meeting a soul mate. Your heart opens, making it easier to express your feelings, especially with children.

Snowflake Obsidian
A reconciliation in an affair of the heart brings much joy. In times of stress and despair, try to make time for pleasure to uplift your spirits.

Snow Quartz
Ensure your pursuit of pleasure is not at the expense of others. Question your motives with regard to a romance.

Unakite
Allow time for pleasurable pursuits which fulfil you spiritually, mentally and emotionally. Let your inner child guide you in play.

Health

SERVICE

HARMONY

HEALING

BALANCE

Caduceus

Well

The sixth life area relates to all aspects of health, not just physical, but also emotional, spiritual and mental well-being. Health issues surrounding others are included in this area. Another aspect is that of helping others by being of service, possibly in some form of healing.

What is inhibiting you from having a full and vital lifestyle, filled with vibrant good health? Are there deep seated fears holding you back in some way? Is it time for you to develop your natural healing gifts?

Crystals in this life area can put you on notice to take greater care of your health. Also, latent healing gifts may be indicated, which it is now time for you to develop. You may be reminded of how you can serve and help others.

THE SYMBOLS

Discriminating *Virgo*, the perfectionist of the zodiac, and the analytical planet *Mercury* remind us of the need to consider carefully issues of health and how to remain in balance with life. The *Caduceus* is recognized as the ancient and traditional universal emblem of healing. It shows the duality and union of oppos-ing forces – balance of mind and body. The *Well* is the source of life-giving water, which refreshes and cleanses. Essential for survival as one of the body's main components, water is a universal

source of energy. The *Red Cross Flag* is recog-nized worldwide as a symbol of aid and hope – the red cross appears throughout history as an emblem of peace and honour. The *Runner* shows the sense of well-being which is attained through physical and sporting activities. Movement can become a form of meditation – move the body to still the mind – start exercising now. *Yin–Yang* is one of the most ancient and widely recognized Eastern symbols for duality, balance and harmony, the uniting opposites which each have a seed of the other within them. The rune *Sigel* symbolizes the life force originating in the sun's energy, as well as vitality, health and regeneration at the cellular level.

When crystals bridge the fifth and sixth life areas you are reminded to try to find pleasure and joy whilst working in service to others. The sixth and seventh areas indicate the possibility of working in harmony with another, in a way that is both fulfilling and of help to others.

Red Cross Flag

Runner

Yin–Yang

Virgo

Mercury

Sigel

THE LIFE CHALLENGE

In order to truly understand something, you must experience it personally. Through personal experience you gain mastery of your power. The test is to allow the difficult and challenging experiences in your life to be of service to you.

There is no point in suffering a tragedy if you do not learn and grow from it. How can you use the times of suffering in your life purposefully? Can you find sufficient courage to use personal tragedy to aid your self-discovery process?

CRYSTAL INTERPRETATIONS

Amethyst
Allow yourself time to contemplate, meditate and heal your inner being. Let the transformation process work through all levels of your psyche.

Aventurine
Have you thought of broadening your therapeutic skills? Stretching body, mind and soul might be just the tonic for you now.

Blue Lace Agate
Explore and develop your own gifts of healing at this time. Allow your own healing process to take place and make this a priority in your life.

Citrine
Listen to and be guided by the needs of your body. Now might be a good time to start a new fitness regime.

Clear Quartz
Be clear about your true motives for wishing to help others. Are your physical, mental and emotional states as balanced and clear as they can be?

Gold Tiger Eye
Do not overdo it at the moment – your health may be more fragile than normal. Could you do with a holiday or more rest at this time?

Hematite
Ensure that you meet the needs of your physical body. Bring spirit into matter as you remain linked to the Light and connected to the Earth.

Red Jasper
Address all health matters in a practical way. You may respond well to massage, vitamins, diet or consider taking up some form of physical exercise.

Rose Quartz
Bring in healing qualities and unconditional love when working with others. Love is the greatest healer of all, especially when healing oneself.

Snowflake Obsidian
Seek the message and hidden benefits within patterns of disease or affliction. Prepare for a test of commitment and willingness to serve the Light.

Snow Quartz
Make sure your lifestyle is particularly healthy at this time. Could this be a good time to fast or restrict some unhealthier aspects of your diet.

Unakite
Are you physically, mentally and emotionally in balance at this time? Ensure others are not demanding too much from you.

Partnership

RELATIONSHIPS

CONTRACTS

UNION

MARKIAGE

Wedding Rings   *Handshake*

The seventh life area indicates all aspects of relationships. Both business and romantic partnerships are included within this area of the wheel, and the signing of contracts may be indicated. Balance is a fundamental theme of this area, as well as any aspects of mutual harmony and union in your life. Also, very importantly, this area asks you to look at how you relate to yourself.

Do you accept yourself? Are you able to see the beauty that is already in your life? Is your current relationship one of fantasy – is it a great adventure or is it true love?

Crystals in this area could direct you to look at matters such as the signing of legal contracts. Any type of partnership may show up here, not just a romantic liaison, so look out for opportunities to work happily and profitably with another person or on a joint venture.

THE SYMBOLS

The zodiac sign *Libra*, denoting cooperation and balance, together with the planet *Venus*, which rules relationships and sociability, remind you of the importance of working in balance and harmony with others. *Wedding Rings* symbolize a witnessed union between two people who come together, making a permanent commitment to share their lives – the culminating point of a relationship. The *Handshake* implies a contract or deal agreed and a pledge of honour to work within a partnership as in 'sealed with a hand-

shake'. The *Everlasting Knot* in Celtic tradition, also known as the 'lucky knot' in Chinese tradition, symbolizes eternity, infinity and continuity within the intricacy of a relationship. *Ears of Corn* show the rewards, such as fruitfulness, creativity and awakening, that can be reaped from a positive partnership that is blessed. Within a happy relationship it is possible to nurture and develop qualities such as truth and wisdom. *Threads of Unity* signify two strands coming together, integrating and linking to work for a common purpose – with unified strength, one supports the other. The rune *Geofu* means partnership or union, both in love and business, and can denote a marriage or engagement.

The sixth and seventh areas indicate the possibility of working in harmony with another, in a way that is both fulfilling and of help to others. The seventh and eighth life areas encourage you to look at the deeper, more mystical significances and karmic implications of your relationships.

Everlasting Knot

Ears of Corn

Threads of Unity

Libra

Venus

Geofu

THE LIFE CHALLENGE

The seventh life area challenges you to learn how to share and lovingly cooperate with others. Whilst learning to be harmonious as you share your life, are you able to maintain your distinctiveness and individuality?

Can you remain true to yourself, expressing your values with purity and truth? Can you retain your power without taking power from others? The test is to remain truly individual and yet not be different or set apart from others.

CRYSTAL INTERPRETATIONS

Amethyst
A turning point is indicated in the way you relate to others. A relationship issue may now be brought to a head.

Aventurine
If thinking of entering a partnership, ensure it helps you grow personally. Someone may enter your life who could be helpful and supportive to you.

Blue Lace Agate
There is the possibility of a relationship which may profoundly affect your life. Partnerships are well aspected if both parties contribute equally.

Citrine
An opportunity for a special partnership might present itself soon. Allow your partner to be a source of inspiration for you now.

Clear Quartz
Make sure you clearly communicate with partners. Reflect on what it is you want from a relationship and perhaps restructure current partnerships.

Gold Tiger Eye
Seek expert advice and take care if signing partnership documents. You may be involved with someone who needs protecting.

Hematite
Relationships formed now will help you to fulfil your spiritual role on Earth – they might not be permanent. Connections with others may involve strong karmic links.

Red Jasper
Let your relationships be more mundane at this time. Seek real down-to-earth partners rather than romantic ideals.

Rose Quartz
Does your partner need to feel loved, accepted and forgiven? Is this a time to balance and reconcile the energies between you and another?

Snowflake Obsidian
Now is the time to reconcile and heal old wounds within a partnership. Try to see the good in others, however negative they may first appear.

Snow Quartz
A spiritual union could be indicated at this time. Carefully check that all contracts are clear and reflect your highest standards.

Unakite
Are your relationships meeting the needs of both partners? Ensure that you are being flexible enough within a relationship.

Mysticism

SUPERSTITIONS

OCCULT

REINCARNATION

BIRTH AND REBIRTH

Mystic Star   *Will and Testament*

The eighth life area relates to every single fundamental life issue you can encounter – birth, sexuality, death, rebirth, hidden fears and the great mysteries of the Universe! It implies an acceptance of mortality, and may point to issues surrounding inheritances, legacies and financial matters.

A re you being challenged to examine your beliefs relating to the issues raised by this area? Is it time to reflect on what the meaning of life is for you?

Crystals here can indicate times of intense re-evaluation and internal meditation. You may be guided to jettison philosophies that have been with you for many years – they may become irrelevant as you undergo a spiritual rebirth.

THE SYMBOLS

Combine the intense and passionate energies of the zodiac sign *Scorpio* with the transformative and regenerative powers of the planet *Pluto* to allow your own rebirth to take place. The seven-pointed *Mystic Star* inspires and elevates – it can become your guiding star. Once the ancient mystics' symbol of prophecy and blessings, it was later adopted by the Christian faith. *Will and Testament* symbolizes inheritance – the passing on of guidance and possessions, and a willingness to contribute a legacy both to individuals and the world. The *Kabbalah*, often referred to as the 'tree of

life', is a map of deep-rooted wisdom – this ancient Jewish philosophy guides those who study the mysteries of life. The *Phoenix*, sometimes known as the 'firebird', appears in Egyptian myth and Mesopotamian iconography. It is the sacred bird who is consumed by fire and then rises up from its own ashes – it symbolizes the eternal renewal of life and immortality of the soul. The *Alchemist's Rose* represents the heart centre which holds the secrets to the mysteries of life, manifested as the sacred marriage of spirit and matter. Divine alchemy operates when death of the ego occurs, transforming dense matter into subtle energy. The rune *Othel* denotes property or possessions passed through generations.

Crystals covering the seventh and eighth life areas encourage you to look at the deeper, more mystical significances and the karmic implications of your relationships. When the eighth and ninth areas are aspected, ensure your journeys result in an expansion of your spiritual horizons.

Kabbalah

Phoenix

Alchemist's Rose

Scorpio

Pluto

Othel

THE LIFE CHALLENGE

Learn to take absolute responsibility for what you create and each and every action you take. The challenge is to understand that each action has a reaction and affects all other beings within the Universe.

Are you willing to accept the role karma may play in your life? Whether you are responsible for the birth of an idea or an invention, or are the creator of a concept, can you carry the burden of responsibility?

CRYSTAL INTERPRETATIONS

Amethyst
Sudden and dramatic illumination could occur at this time. You may instantly discover what, for you, is the meaning of life.

Aventurine
Exploring the psyche and the mystical aspects of nature helps even with everyday matters. You might be due for an inheritance in some form at this time.

Blue Lace Agate
Influences from the past will make their presence felt now. Make sure that your personal affairs and the affairs of those close to you are all in order.

Citrine
Listen to your Divine guidance and act upon it! It may be an appropriate time for you to delve deeper into the mysteries of life.

Clear Quartz
You may need to clarify your part in the universal plan of life and discover its significance. Allow yourself to explore the more mystical aspects of life.

Gold Tiger Eye
If tempted to explore the more mystical aspects of life, ensure you are expertly guided. Be careful with any aspects that involve the occult.

Hematite
Explore your destiny and spiritual mission in this life. Make time to study the mysteries of life in a disciplined and structured way.

Red Jasper
True spirituality is being able to anchor the Light within the physical realm. Let the past and future inspire you, but live absolutely in the now.

Rose Quartz
Apply a higher wisdom to understand the universal patterns that occur within life. Accept and learn from past mistakes, then forgive yourself and move on.

Snowflake Obsidian
Let realization slowly dawn within your consciousness. Allow Light to fill your life – you do not need to chase it or make anything happen.

Snow Quartz
Ensure that you are working at the highest spiritual level you are capable of at this time. Examine your motives to make sure they are pure.

Unakite
Develop your spiritual being without losing touch with reality. Move on from what is safe and familiar one step at a time into a new awareness.

Travel

JOURNEYS

EXPANDING HORIZONS

ADVENTURE

FURTHER KNOWLEDGE

Rising Sun

Labyrinth

The ninth life area relates to travel in all senses of the word. It can mean long-distance travelling to exciting destinations. Likewise this can also include broadening of the mind, so going to college to study could equally well be indicated in this area.

Do you want to broaden your horizons in some way? Is it time for a holiday? Do you need to take a break and look at issues from afar? Is it time for you to start a search for the meaning of your life?

Crystals falling into this area may give you clues as to which direction to take. You may be reminded to broaden your perspective. It could be time to stand back and review your life. Allow your mind to journey and explore the Universe.

THE SYMBOLS

The adventurous and freedom-loving zodiac sign of *Sagittarius* and expansive, benevolent planet, *Jupiter*, encourage us to explore new realms in order to gain a deeper understanding of this Universe. The *Rising Sun* appearing on the horizon shows the limitless possibilities available to you as you travel. Expand your own inner horizons and you explore new possibilities and fresh ideas. The *Labyrinth* symbolizes your inner journey of discovery as you travel through life's maze – each person has to walk the convoluted path

of enlightenment in their own unique way. The *Compass* encourages you to look out for spiritual signposts which will be there to help you navigate, showing you the starting point, how far you have travelled and a way towards the final destination. The *Galleon* is an expression of the perilous journey through life. Transformation takes place as you make safe passage across the sea of life through uncharted water, successfully overcoming the challenges. The *Travel Bag* reminds you to collect experiences in life and carry them with you to give further insight; but beware of unnecessary burdens which might impede your progress – travel light! The rune *Rad* symbolizes journeying and communication and powerful thought patterns.

When the eighth and ninth areas are aspected, ensure your journeys result in an expansion of your spiritual horizons. A combination of the ninth and tenth life areas suggests you look at how you can integrate your career with travel.

Compass

Galleon

Travel Bag

Sagittarius

Jupiter

Rad

THE LIFE CHALLENGE

Bring sense and significance to your journey and knowledge. How can you discover the spiritual meaning of what you have learned so far? There is little point in studying unless you give spiritual meaning to the knowledge you gain.

Can you now transform your knowledge and experience into wisdom? Ensure your life journey has spiritual meaning – travel purposefully, check that you are not running away – above all enjoy the journey.

CRYSTAL INTERPRETATIONS

Amethyst
Move away from usual routines and usual rhythms of life to experience the winds of change. Perhaps it is time for a spiritual pilgrimage.

Aventurine
Let yourself go, feel free to travel as much as possible now. Through greater knowledge you can liberate yourself.

Blue Lace Agate
Avoid ecstatic highs as inevitably lows follow – do everything in moderation. Try to keep travel plans in perspective and avoid extremes.

Citrine
Seek a light-filled holiday location to replenish your body and your soul. Study subjects which lift your spirits and inspire you.

Clear Quartz
Expand your mind and spiritual perspective by travelling to other dimensions. Discard old habits and emotional debris to see clearly your way forward.

Gold Tiger Eye
Travel plans are not everything they seem – allow extra time. Expand your awareness of life slowly – there is no need to rush into anything.

Hematite
You are being inevitably drawn to a spiritual turning point. Surrender to the higher will of the Divine and accept your destiny as you travel through life.

Red Jasper
Longed-for dreams may finally come true at this time. Allow yourself to undertake that journey or adventure of a lifetime.

Rose Quartz
Enjoy expanding your belief system as you make your spiritual journey in life. Choose the travel destinations you want – please yourself, not others.

Snowflake Obsidian
Feel yourself being guided as you walk along your path travelling towards the Light. A very special journey may take place at this time.

Snow Quartz
A journey could bring about a profound change within the spiritual dimensions of your life. Allow for the unexpected with all travel plans.

Unakite
Aim to mix business with pleasure when you travel. Study that which fascinates you mentally and enthralls you emotionally.

Career

ASPIRATIONS

POWER

FAME

PUBLIC IMAGE

Ladder   *Target*

The tenth life area looks at your public persona – how you are perceived by the world – as well as all career and business matters. Authority issues will show up here as will your relationship to society via occupational activities. Potential for the misuse of power may be highlighted in this area.

Does your work life satisfy you at all levels? If not, how can you change this? Are you being prompted to make a significant career move or is it time to rest, withdraw or make a dramatic change? Can you be trusted with power or could ambition overtake integrity?

Crystals in this life area encourage you to accept your power and authority, particularly in public. You may develop your leadership skills or receive some form of public recognition.

THE SYMBOLS

The industrious and ambitious zodiac sign of *Capricorn* together with *Saturn*, the planet of structure and responsibility, guide you to attain and use power wisely for the good of humanity. The *Ladder* shows you climbing up or down in your career. Remember to step on each rung; if you miss one you may need to go back and take that step again. The *Target* helps you focus and aim for the centre so that your arrow of ambition can take flight to hit the bull's-eye – all essential ingredients to success. *Mountains* symbolize

your aspirations and dreams. There may be peaks and troughs involving hard and challenging climbs, but the possibilities are infinite – the sky is the limit as you know you can reach the pinnacle. The *Crown* is a universal symbol of ruler-ship, power and authority, ideally combined with wisdom and honour. Ennobled status rewards those with high ideals, dedication and a sense of responsibility for others. *Tools of the Trade* are the medium through which you can manifest your ideas and thoughts. They imply that you have served your apprenticeship and earned the right, through hard work, to succeed. The rune *Ing* represents the possibility of starting a new trade, the birth of a project or the successful completion of a plan.

A combination of the ninth and tenth life areas suggests you look at how you can integrate your career with travel. The tenth and eleventh blend to encourage you to develop work situations within the community and with groups of people.

Mountains

Crown

Tools of the Trade

Capricorn

Saturn

Ing

THE LIFE CHALLENGE

You are challenged to look at how you participate in life and uphold your position in society. Do you act responsibly, honour your position and deserve the trust bestowed upon you or do you abuse the power you have at your disposal?

The true leader ensures that the strong support and empower the weak. You have earned the right to the status and the responsibility it carries. Can you now become a point of light and shining example for those still existing in darkness?

CRYSTAL INTERPRETATIONS

Amethyst
Others will now see you in a different light and may comment on it. Allow yourself to be moved into positions of authority if the opportunity arises.

Aventurine
Now is a time to allow yourself to aspire to the highest level – let your true ambitions guide you. Are you working in the way that really fulfils you?

Blue Lace Agate
Do not be too rash if tempted to cut free from commitments and old ties. You will receive the recognition and rewards you richly deserve in time.

Citrine
Inject more enthusiasm into your work life and be abundantly rewarded. Now the sky is the limit for your ambitions – do not limit yourself!

Clear Quartz
Clearly state your needs, aims and ambitions at work. Do not allow yourself to be limited in your career at this time.

Gold Tiger Eye
Double check and check again before signing contracts or making commitments. Could you or a colleague need to be extra cautious at work – watch out!

Hematite
Openly express your beliefs even to those less sympathetic. Past endeavours will create beneficial opportunities.

Red Jasper
You can make things happen at work. Your ambitions and long-term plans can now come to fruition.

Rose Quartz
How can more harmony and balance be brought into your workplace? Colleagues may need extra understanding and forgiveness to reconcile difficult situations.

Snowflake Obsidian
Allow your power to shine through at work. Now is the time to make a stand and take up your rightful position.

Snow Quartz
Ensure work standards are legally and ethically acceptable. A major promotion or change of emphasis could occur in your work life.

Unakite
Whenever possible, enjoy the work you do and enhance your work environment. Allow your heart to guide your ambitions.

Community

FRIENDSHIP

GROUP OBJECTIVES

ASSOCIATIONS

GLOBAL ISSUES

Beehive

Olympic Insignia

The eleventh life area relates to groups of people. This might mean groups you work, study or play with. It could also refer to your own neighbourhood and community. Your relationships with friends and the way you interact with groups of people will arise here. Also your relationship with the global community and the human race as a family is an aspect of this area.

What group connections enhance your identity? How does your behaviour differ when you are with a group of people to when you are on your own? Are your friendships mutually supportive?

Crystals here may encourage you to participate in group projects. You might be reminded that development and learning often flourish in a group situation. You may find your awareness of group issues is raised at this time and you start to feel part of the great universal whole.

THE SYMBOLS

Aquarius is the zodiac sign of humanitarianism and *Uranus* the planet of innovations and rebellion; together they guide us to hold a wider vision and change society for the better. The *Beehive* symbolizes perfectly the community spirit with each individual cooperating with others in the group to achieve a common goal. The *Olympic Insignia*, the interlinked rings, represents the Olympic dream of people living, working and competing together – one people

aspiring together to keep alive the flame of life which lights the way for the human race. The *Global Recycling* symbol is a reminder to 'think globally – act locally'. One small act on the part of one human will ultimately affect every individual on the planet. Recycling is a universal pattern; everything is eventually recycled. The *World Peace* symbol represents the potential for a global village; when there are parallel links between different cultures and no boundaries, the spirit of universal peace can reside on Earth. The *Human Family* shows humanity as one race, connected to support each other on all levels, linking hands, thought and energy to the group. The rune *Mann* symbolizes the interdependence of humanity and humankind working together as one race.

The tenth and eleventh life areas blend to encourage you to develop work situations within the community and with groups of people. The eleventh and twelfth inspire you to transcend existing visions and expand your perception.

Global Recycling

World Peace

Human Family

Aquarius

Uranus

Mann

THE LIFE CHALLENGE

The challenge is to use feelings of discontent you may have with a system or situation to fuel growth and change. Explore how you can bring about creative progress for humanity either within a community or at a more global level.

There needs to be an increase in inclusiveness and a collective working for the greater good of the universal whole. Are you able to take on the role of social responsibility and leadership to bring about positive change?

CRYSTAL INTERPRETATIONS

Amethyst
Harness the group energy to help you step into a changed state of being. A meditation or spiritual development group may be helpful at this time.

Aventurine
Let your conscience guide your actions. You might be able to make a valuable contribution to charity at this time and reap rewards yourself.

Blue Lace Agate
Think globally and act locally. Balance the needs of your community and your commitments to group issues with those of your close family.

Citrine
You could be the centre of attention within a group activity. Did you know that your words and actions could inspire others?

Clear Quartz
Share your light with your peers, group members and local community. Your confidence may grow when you work on projects with groups of people.

Gold Tiger Eye
Be cautious with group activities; make sure everyone does their fair share. Does a community or group project need to be guarded and watched over?

Hematite
Join a well-structured group enterprise to ensure that you are expertly guided and supported. Realize a personal goal within a group environment.

Red Jasper
A group may give you additional strength and resources. With the help of a friend, events can unfold in line with your part of the cosmic plan.

Rose Quartz
Groups situations and experiences bring you luck, acceptance and balance. Look to group connections and projects for friendship and spiritual development.

Snowflake Obsidian
Leadership qualities within group situations may emerge now. Start working with a group that actively brings light into dark situations on Earth.

Snow Quartz
Become a catalyst within a group to raise standards and aspirations. Does something in your neighbourhood need cleansing and purifying?

Unakite
Encourage friends from different walks of life to meet and share with one another. Can you participate in a group project which heals others and yourself?

Philosophy

KARMA

FATE

SUBCONSCIOUS

SECRET SELF

Eagle

Shadow Man

The twelfth life area deals with those parts of our lives which we are least in touch with. The collective consciousness, your part in the greater plan and subconscious issues will show up here. You may wish to examine your true spiritual beliefs and values. Also, your philosophical attitudes to religion, meditation and the divine connection are all encompassed within this life area.

Are you able to tap into your subconscious and make the knowledge held there conscious? Is it time for your spiritual aspect to triumph over physical matter?

Crystals that fall in this area might ask you to face your 'shadow side'. It takes great courage to enter the hidden depths that reside within the dark side, but your efforts will yield abundant spiritual rewards. Look at what is going on beneath the surface of your consciousness. Also explore dreams, areas of fantasy, and karma – the spiritual law of cause and effect.

THE SYMBOLS

The impressionable and imaginative zodiac sign of *Pisces* and the nebulous and illusory planet *Neptune* help us to get in touch with the mystical aspects of life. The *Eagle* is a universal symbol of transcendence and power. It represents the expansion and elevation of the soul as it soars above the material world. *Shadow Man* represents the inner self, secrets and positive qualities. The shadow aspect often contains fears as well

as creative impulsiveness – it can overshadow uncomfortable aspects as well as lighten them. The *Ankh*, Egyptian hieroglyphic of eternal life, is a key to the hidden mysteries of Heaven and Earth – it anchors the Light, wisdom and power on Earth. The *Hidden Mind* suggests opening up to new concepts and exploration of the inner realms of the mind; the seed of consciousness or soul is often considered to reside in the head. The *Rainbow Chalices* represent the link between conscious and subconscious, Heaven and Earth; follow your rainbow to find the chalice, which is the grail or spiritual treasure, hidden within you. The rune *Yr* symbolizes the yew tree which is a sign of the evolution of the soul.

The eleventh and twelfth life areas inspire you to transcend existing visions and expand your perception. Crystals spanning the twelfth and first life areas remind you to ensure the beliefs you express and portray to the world are truly your own and relevant to you at this time in your life.

Ankh

Hidden Mind

Rainbow Chalices

Pisces

Neptune

Yr

THE LIFE CHALLENGE

The challenge of the twelfth life area is to distinguish between that which is immortal and that which must end and disintegrate. Are you able to perceive that which belongs to the realm of timeless spirit?

You are challenged to understand the true nature of death. Can you allow the transfiguration process to take place within you? As you allow the death of one phase of life, learn that this preludes the birth of a new cycle.

CRYSTAL INTERPRETATIONS

Amethyst
Prayer and meditation will help you make the transitions that occur at this time. Let go of old and redundant thought patterns.

Aventurine
Make time to meditate to help expand your mind and spirit. Express your innermost secrets and hidden aspects of your psyche in a safe space.

Blue Lace Agate
Accept your shadow side – allow yourself to be imperfect sometimes! Let your enlightenment process unfold – you do not need to try so hard.

Citrine
Listen to your intuition and be guided by your inner knowing. Can you meld the spiritual into the physical aspects of your life?

Clear Quartz
Let light shine deep into your inner being to allow exploration of the subconscious. As more light shines into your being, the shadow side is also emphasized.

Gold Tiger Eye
What often seems real is in fact illusory, it is just a question of perception. Are you guided by your subconscious desires or your rational thoughts?

Hematite
Learn how to anchor the Light within your whole being. Harmonize your spiritual life within your physical life.

Red Jasper
Dreams can now become reality with just a little practical help from you. Try to incorporate your inner truth with your outer, worldly, day-to-day life.

Rose Quartz
Although not always easy, trust and surrender to the vibration of unconditional love. Resonate at the deepest level of your being to the Love Wisdom ray.

Snowflake Obsidian
You can experience a deep sense of enlightenment and spiritual inspiration at this time. Allow yourself to be guided by your own spiritual truth and values.

Snow Quartz
Events happening now may be due to your past actions. 'As above, so below', even your unconscious thoughts could be affecting your life now.

Unakite
Can you make the final commitment of a spiritual marriage, uniting spirit and matter? Can you now anchor the Light into earthly reality?

Sample Reading

Patricia is seeking employment having been made redundant from her job as an administrator in the legal profession. She is in her late twenties, currently single and focusing much of her life on a possible career change. She also wishes to develop her new found interest in spiritual matters and complementary medicine. She wants an overview of her life as she feels there is a certain amount of confusion and conflict.

CASTING ONTO THE LIFE WHEEL

Patricia asks, 'What influences are active in my life at this time?' whilst choosing five crystals from the pouch. She selects **Blue Lace Agate** *(harmonization)*, **Citrine** *(inspiration)*, **Clear Quartz** *(clarification)*, **Gold Tiger Eye** *(protection)* and **Snowflake Obsidian** *(illumination)*. She then concentrates on the question, 'Where do I need to focus these influences?' and casts the crystals onto the Life Wheel. They indicate the following life areas and symbols: Blue Lace Agate falls in the second life area, **Prosperity**, on the *Coin*; Citrine falls in the third life area, **Communication**, on the *Work of Art*; Clear Quartz falls in the second life area, **Prosperity**, on the *Norse Money Charm*; Gold Tiger Eye falls in the ninth life area, **Travel**, on the *Galleon*; Snowflake Obsidian falls in the eleventh life area, **Community**, on the rune *Mann*.

THE INTERPRETATION

Blue Lace Agate and **Clear Quartz** in the second life area of **Prosperity** indicate a need for Patricia to focus on what makes her feel secure and stable in this life and also suggest she might look at personal values and financial issues. The money aspect of this life area seems to be highlighted by the two symbols aspected by the crystals – the *Coin* and the *Norse Money Charm*. Blue Lace Agate suggests that she accepts her material needs and appreciates what she actually has.

Patricia is advised to balance the need to save for the future with having sufficient resources to live for today. Clear Quartz suggests that she clarifies her values and asks herself what she holds to be truly dear and important. It is recommended that she bring some structure into the material part of her life.

Citrine falling in the third life area of **Communication** suggests a need to look at creative issues, ensuring that she is communicating effectively and expressing what she wants to others. As the Citrine has fallen onto the *Work of Art*, this especially emphasizes a need to express creatively. It is time for Patricia to express herself with great enthusiasm and clarity. She has the ability to inspire others when she communicates.

Gold Tiger Eye in the ninth life area of **Travel** cautions Patricia to take care when travelling long distances and seeking further knowledge. It has fallen on the *Galleon* which symbolizes the life journey and possibly suggests that she should not over-extend herself at this time with regard to spiritual development. Travel plans are not everything they seem – extra time should be allowed. She should expand her awareness of life slowly – there is no need to rush into anything. This reiterates the message given in the symbolism of the *Galleon*.

Snowflake Obsidian in the eleventh life area of **Community** encourages Patricia to look for the positive and helpful qualities which may lie within group endeavours and projects. It has fallen on the rune *Mann* which symbolizes the interdependence of humanity and humankind working together as one race. Leadership qualities within group situations may occur now. Patricia may feel drawn to working with a group that actively brings light into dark situations on Earth.

SUMMARY

Patricia is advised to recognize and accept that financial matters are important to her, possibly they help her to feel safe and secure. These needs should not be ignored when considering changes in career. It is also indicated that a creative outlet is necessary at this time. She should try to find a pursuit which inspires her and gives clarity of vision. It is important that she makes time for this in her life. It may be helpful to seek out a group of like-minded people who share her desire to expand awareness. This would be mutually supportive; however, the slower pace that such a group may enforce would have to be accepted. Patricia is advised not to try to develop her spirituality alone at this time. There is no need to rush anything – there is plenty of time.

CRYSTAL CASTING

Patricia asks: 'What influences are active in my life at this time?'
She selects five crystals.
Patricia then asks: 'Where do I need to focus these influences?'
She then casts the crystals.

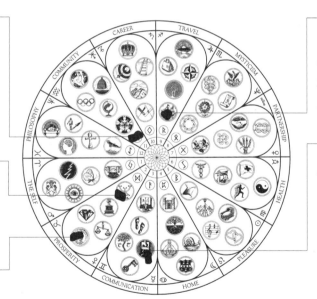

Snowflake Obsidian on the rune Mann in the eleventh life area of Community suggests seeking positive and helpful qualities which may lie within group endeavours.

Clear Quartz on the Norse Money Charm in the second life area of Prosperity asks that personal values are clarified at this time.

Blue Lace Agate on the Coin in the second life area of Prosperity implies a need to focus on financial issues.

Gold Tiger Eye on the Galleon in the ninth life area of Travel indicates a need for caution when travelling long distances or seeking further knowledge.

Citrine on the Work of Art in the third life area of Communication points towards a need to look at creative issues.

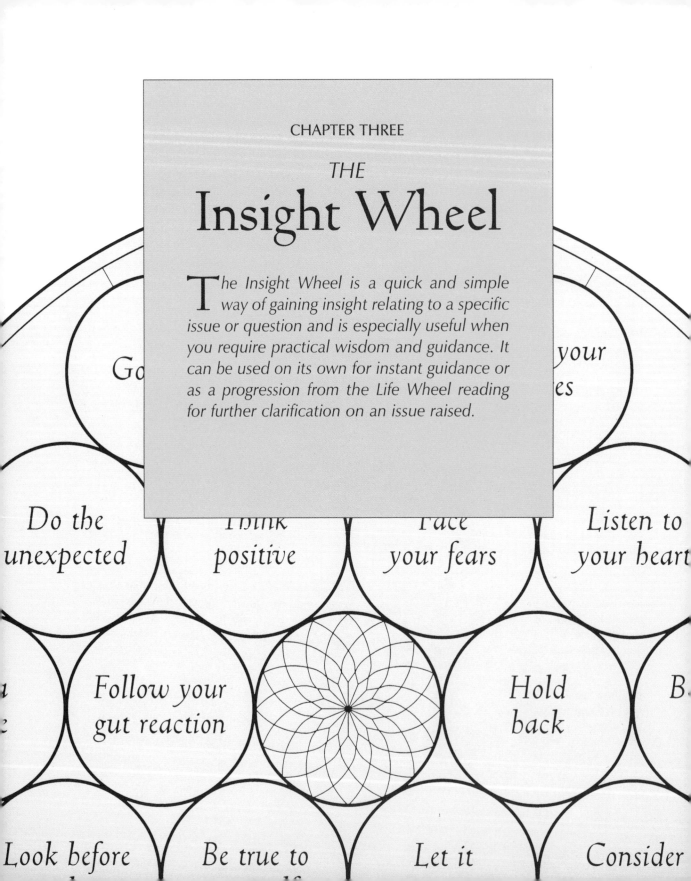

CHAPTER THREE

THE

Insight Wheel

The Insight Wheel is a quick and simple way of gaining insight relating to a specific issue or question and is especially useful when you require practical wisdom and guidance. It can be used on its own for instant guidance or as a progression from the Life Wheel reading for further clarification on an issue raised.

Go

your

es

Do the
unexpected

Think
positive

Face
your fears

Listen to
your heart

Follow your
gut reaction

Hold
back

B

Look before

Be true to

Let it

Consider

How to use the Insight Wheel

By clearly thinking of a specific question or issue while selecting your crystals from the pouch, you will attract the guidance and insight you need.

You can receive up to three self-explanatory messages; these will be indicated by the positions of the crystals cast. The aim is to give insight and guidance, not yes or no answers.

GETTING THE MOST FROM THE INSIGHT WHEEL

PHRASING THE QUESTION

Firstly, it is essential to phrase the question correctly. If you are reading for someone else, it is advisable to ask them to tell you the question before you start. This ensures that it is not a question which needs to be answered with a 'yes' or 'no'. Remember, the wheel gives insight, not yes or no answers.

Ideal questions might be:

'I need guidance on whether to undertake training as a counsellor/accountant.'

'Give me insight with regard to my proposed trip abroad.'

'I would like to know how my past will help me in my present situation.'

'I need clarification on whether to take that new job/make a career move.'

'Can I have insight on how to resolve the dispute between myself and my neighbour/friend?'

'I need insight on how to best help my friend/colleague/partner/brother.'

'I need insight and guidance with regard to my relationship with …'

Avoid questions such as, 'Will I benefit at this time from training as a counsellor/accountant?' or 'Should I go on holiday abroad this year?' Also, questions such as, 'Which training course would be best for me?' or 'Which holiday destination should I choose?' will not work with the Insight Wheel!

You can continue asking questions of the Insight Wheel, reselecting and recasting the stones each time. The crystals will tell you when it is no longer appropriate by falling outside the wheel.

FOCUSING ON THE QUESTION

The greater degree of concentration and focus on the question when selecting and casting the crystals, the more accurate and appropriate the answers will be. You can try speaking the question out loud as you choose and cast the crystals. Also, try writing the question down beforehand. For more detailed instructions on how to prepare for making a reading, see the instructions for using the Life Wheel *(pages 27–31).*

CASTING ONTO THE INSIGHT WHEEL

1. With eyes closed, focus clearly on the question or issue and select three crystals from the pouch.

2. Note which crystals have been selected as this will help later on with your interpretation.

3. Still focusing on the question, hold the crystals between the palms of your hands approximately 5–8 centimetres (2–3 inches) above the centre of the wheel and cast the crystals by letting them drop onto the wheel, or cast

them in the way which feels right for you.

4. Note which insight spheres are indicated and by which crystals. Then, using the Guidelines for Interpretation, draw guidance from the Insight Wheel.

5. If you wish to ask another question, return all the crystals to the pouch and mix them around before selecting new stones.

GUIDELINES FOR INTERPRETATION

POSITION OF THE CRYSTALS

Any crystals which fall outside the wheel should be put to one side and disregarded. If a crystal falls in the central sphere then the theme of the crystal should be considered and combined with the other answers. When two or more stones fall within the same sphere the answer indicated is particularly strong and important.

Sometimes, two spheres may be indicated by one crystal falling across them. Wherever possible, try to move the crystal into the sphere that seems to dominate. On the rare occasion when the crystal equally spans the two spheres, consider both answers equally.

If all three crystals fall outside the wheel, rephrase the question and re-cast the crystals. If the crystals still do not fall onto the wheel, please accept it is not appropriate for you to ask this question at this time.

INTERPRETING THE MESSAGE

The crystals are used primarily to indicate a particular part of the wheel which gives a simple phrase of guidance. However, the three stones chosen will also contribute to the answer as they each carry their own theme and influence. When you have selected your three crystals you may wish to look up their possible significances on the relevant pages in Chapter Two (see pages 14–25).

By considering the theme of the crystal, it is possible to add more light and shade to your answers. It is also helpful to consider which crystals have been selected, as they will subtly alter the nuance of the insight messages they fall on – look at how the qualities indicated by the stone enhance the answer within the sphere. For example, if 'Be on your guard' were indicated by **Gold Tiger Eye** (keyword: protection), the message is doubly strong. However, if indicated by **Clear Quartz** (keyword: clarification), it may be advising to take greater care to ensure everyone is clear about a situation, everything is clearly understood and not to take anything for granted. If 'Listen to your Heart' is aspected by **Rose Quartz**, this suggests that something dear to you needs reconciling. Whereas if **Snowflake Obsidian** highlights this message, it indicates that following your heart's desire could lead to illumination.

Occasionally seemingly contradictory answers may be given such as, 'Go for it', and 'Not now'. This could be indicating that a proposed project is positively aspected but now is not the right time. 'Hold back' and 'Let it go' might suggest that you need to personally stand back from involvement in a project or job and release it to someone else. Usually the choice of crystals will help clarify any such contradictions.

USING WITH THE LIFE WHEEL

If using the Insight Wheel after a Life Wheel reading (see pages 27–31), note particularly any crystals which recur and, if possible, recall what those crystals were indicating in the Life Wheel reading, as these may have special relevance. Remember, it is always helpful to keep a written record of your readings.

SUGGESTED THEMES AND INFLUENCES OF THE TWELVE CRYSTALS

AMETHYST

Amethyst brings themes of change to a situation, shifts in consciousness and transformation. Whatever the action – whether you 'Take a chance' or 'Consider patience' – ultimately the situation will have a transformational resolution.

AVENTURINE

Aventurine suggests an influence of broadened vision, increased knowledge and expansion. Whether you are guided to 'Be on your guard' or 'Do the unexpected', ensure that you explore and look at the wider picture.

BLUE LACE AGATE

This stone imparts an influence of healing, balance and harmony. You may be guided to 'Go for it' or 'Be unconventional', but nonetheless your actions will bring harmony to the situation.

CITRINE

Citrine suggests you allow yourself to become inspired as you apply possible solutions to a situation. Whether you are urged to 'Face your fears' or 'Listen to your heart', you can expect to be inspirational as you resolve your question.

CLEAR QUARTZ

Carrying a theme of clarity, structure and focus to the issue, Clear Quartz ensures you are 100 per cent clear and committed to your actions whether you are recommended to 'Think positive' or to 'Hold back'!

GOLD TIGER EYE

This stone suggests a need for caution and protection. You may 'Take a chance' or 'Dare to be different' but look out for unexpected or deceptive influences – do not take anything at face value!

HEMATITE

This crystal suggests something is destined or preordained in a situation. Bear in mind this theme of inevitability whether the 'Not now' message advises you to put plans on hold, or you are encouraged to 'Explore new avenues'.

RED JASPER

Red Jasper conveys a theme of practicality. If you need to 'Follow your desires' manifest this with actions and deeds, do not just think about it. If you need to 'Hold back' then take no action whatsoever, avoid half-hearted responses.

ROSE QUARTZ

This gentle crystal brings love energy, showing the possibility of healing and reconciliation. Resolution to a dilemma may occur whether you 'Dare to be different' or 'Be true to yourself'.

SNOWFLAKE OBSIDIAN

Snowflake Obsidian reveals light at the end of the tunnel and reminds you of the silver lining within every cloud. Look at a situation with illumination, whether you are directed to 'Follow your gut reaction' or 'Look before you leap'.

SNOW QUARTZ

This stone cleanses and clears away old issues and redundant patterns surrounding a dilemma. As you 'Think positive' or 'Take a chance' do so with purity of motivation and purpose in order to wipe the slate clean and have a fresh start.

UNAKITE

Unakite suggests different strands of energy need to meld and blend into one harmonious whole. Allow a unification process to take place, whether you need to 'Be on your guard' or 'Let it go'.

Sample Reading

Cassandra is a thirty-five-year-old married social worker. She feels it is the right time for her and her husband to buy their own home. Her husband is hesitating, as he is concerned about the financial implications and this is now becoming a source of conflict between them. She wants to return, when she has more time, for a full reading to look at the wider picture, but in the meantime feels she needs some immediate guidance regarding this burning issue.

QUESTION ONE

Cassandra asks, 'Please give me insight regarding my wish for us to buy our own home.' Whilst focusing on this question she selects three crystals from the pouch. She chooses: Snow Quartz (*purification*), Hematite (*preordination*) and Blue Lace Agate (*harmonization*). She then casts the crystals onto the Insight Wheel, still concentrating on the question. Snow Quartz falls on 'Face your fears'; Hematite falls on 'Do the unexpected'; and Blue Lace Agate falls on 'Not now'.

Snow Quartz on 'Face your fears' suggests Cassandra needs to check her underlying motives for wishing to buy a home. Why is it so important to her, especially now? What is the urgency? Is buying a home a mask for a deeper issue?

'Do the unexpected', especially when indicated by Hematite, shows an unconventional approach needs to be taken and yet also seems to say that there is a predestined situation and challenge taking place. She could surprise both herself and her husband by looking at alternatives, perhaps moving house, but not buying outright just yet. Are they looking at the right type of home or area?

'Not now', as indicated by Blue Lace Agate, shows clearly there is a timing factor at work here. She may feel the urgency of the situation, but be a little ahead of herself. Perhaps she needs to give her husband some time to get used to the idea. This is certainly not saying it will not happen, simply to hold fire for a while.

QUESTION TWO

Cassandra then asks a second question focusing more on her relationship with her husband. She asks: 'How can I resolve the dispute between Tom and I?' She replaces the stones in the pouch, shuffles them, then selects three more crystals. She chooses: Unakite (*unification*), Rose Quartz (*reconciliation*) and, once again, Snow Quartz (*purification*); she feels these keywords are particularly relevant to her situation. She then casts the crystals: Snow Quartz falls on 'Be true to yourself'; Rose Quartz falls on 'Hold back'; and Unakite falls on 'Look before you leap'.

As Snow Quartz appears again, this seems to be a key crystal. Initially it advised Cassandra to face her fears, now it suggests a need to be true to herself. She needs to look within at what she really wants from her relationship. The Unakite certainly seems to say that in order for a unification of energies to take place, careful consideration should be given prior to any actions being taken. This is further reinforced by the 'Hold back' message indicated by the Rose Quartz.

SUMMARY

Interestingly the second casting seems to echo the first. Cassandra needs to look within first of all at what she wants and needs in her life and put any actions on hold. It does seem more than possible for there to be a reconciliation and a union, but first Cassandra needs to do some soul searching – the answers lie within her.

CRYSTAL CASTING: QUESTION ONE

Cassandra asks: 'Please give me insight regarding my wish for us to buy our own home.'
She selects three crystals from the pouch.
She then casts the crystals, while focusing on the question.

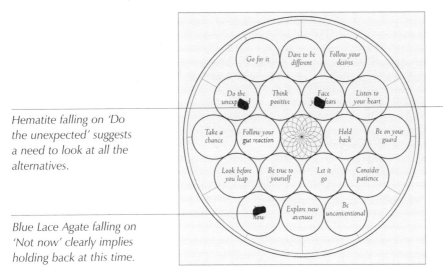

Hematite falling on 'Do the unexpected' suggests a need to look at all the alternatives.

Snow Quartz falling on 'Face your fears' asks Cassandra to check her motives.

Blue Lace Agate falling on 'Not now' clearly implies holding back at this time.

CRYSTAL CASTING: QUESTION TWO

Cassandra asks: 'How can I resolve the dispute between Tom and I?'
She selects three crystals from the pouch.
She then casts the crystals, while focusing on the question.

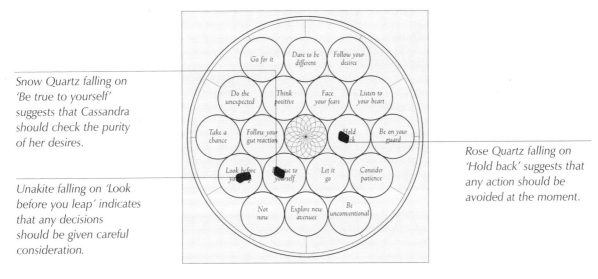

Snow Quartz falling on 'Be true to yourself' suggests that Cassandra should check the purity of her desires.

Rose Quartz falling on 'Hold back' suggests that any action should be avoided at the moment.

Unakite falling on 'Look before you leap' indicates that any decisions should be given careful consideration.

CHAPTER FOUR

THE
Healing Wheel

The Healing Wheel is a reference map of the human energy system. Each one of the nineteen spheres relates to a specific aspect of your energy field. Discover which part of your energy system requires balancing and healing by casting crystals onto the wheel to see which spheres are aspected. The crystals you have selected will give further insight into the type of healing you need.

How it Works

There are nineteen spheres in the wheel representing:

- the seven chakras
- the six realms of consciousness
- the five elements
- the 'All That Is' sphere

These aspects are all represented within you and are, ideally, in a state of balance and harmony. However, it is more usual for some to be in a state of flux and change, especially when healing is required.

You may wish to use the Healing Wheel for self-healing or, as you gain more experience, to offer healing to others, either as part of a reading or in a separate session altogether. It can be used for a general energy balance to bring about harmony and well-being or as a healing tool for a specific condition, feeling or issue. Experienced healers will find this unique healing mandala both fascinating and useful in their professional therapeutic work.

> Important Note: *Please follow the guidelines on pages 67–9 to gain maximum benefit from the Healing Wheel. It is also recommended that you study Chapter Five, Using Crystals for Healing (see pages 100–105) to deepen your understanding and awareness of the healing process which takes place with crystals.*

INTRODUCTION TO THE HEALING SPHERES

There are nineteen spheres in the Healing Wheel; each one relates to a specific aspect of your energy field. They fall into three categories: the chakras, the realms of consciousness, and the elements; as well as the 'All That Is' sphere which encompasses all the spheres. Each sphere correlates to one or more of the other spheres, this is reflected in their arrangement on the Wheel. The groups of spheres are shown below and overleaf in the context of the whole Wheel.

THE SEVEN CHAKRAS

Chakras are centres of concentrated energy which help us to accept, assimilate and give out life force. They are sometimes described as energy transformers, which monitor the amount of energy entering and leaving the physical body and the subtle energy field. The seven chakras are: the Base Chakra, the Sacral Chakra, the Solar Plexus Chakra, the Heart Chakra, the Throat Chakra, the Brow Chakra and the Crown Chakra.

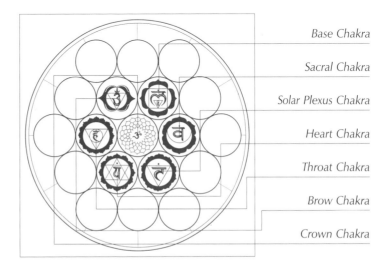

Base Chakra

Sacral Chakra

Solar Plexus Chakra

Heart Chakra

Throat Chakra

Brow Chakra

Crown Chakra

THE SIX REALMS OF CONSCIOUSNESS

There are different fields of experience to which we are all connected. Within each one of us there is a seed pattern which links us to each of the realms: Mineral, Plant, Animal, Human, Planetary and Angelic.

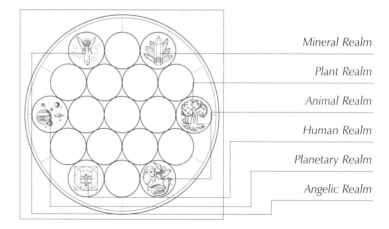

Mineral Realm

Plant Realm

Animal Realm

Human Realm

Planetary Realm

Angelic Realm

THE FIVE ELEMENTS

We are each made up of the five elements – Earth, Water, Air, Fire and Ether. They are always there latently within the energy system but sometimes need to be activated or reawakened.

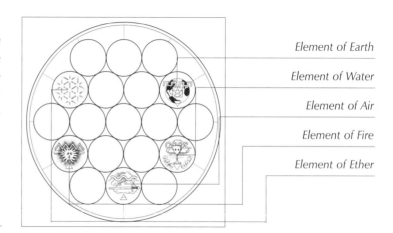

Element of Earth

Element of Water

Element of Air

Element of Fire

Element of Ether

THE 'ALL THAT IS' SPHERE

This sphere is unique and stands alone. It relates to the entire energy system and encompasses the chakras, realms of consciousness and elements.

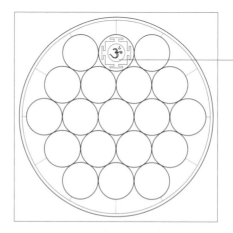

The 'All That Is' Sphere

AN ENERGETIC EXPLANATION

The symbols within the spheres on the Healing Wheel form energy patterns which 'hold' the energy of the element, realm of consciousness or chakra they represent. These energy patterns reflect within you to form a composite pattern which may show up some imbalance, such as excess or deficient energy. Imbalances can occur in one or more of the spheres.

As you cast the crystals, the composite pattern then draws to it the crystalline energy required to make the pattern whole and perfect again. In other words, the energy pattern of the crystal falls into the sphere where it is most needed to restore balance and harmony to that area of your energy system. Crystals hold and enhance certain healing qualities (see pages 12–13). As they are cast onto the Healing Wheel, they can activate a healing frequency and specifically guide it to the area represented by the sphere in which the crystal has 'fallen'.

HOW TO USE THE HEALING WHEEL

PREPARING TO USE THE HEALING WHEEL
This is a similar process to that used for reading the Life Wheel. You will need a comfortable chair to sit in and a table or flat surface for the wheel and crystals. It is strongly recommended that you use a candle – this sets the spiritual vibration and tone for the healing. Please make sure that you are left undisturbed during the healing session.

For the healing to be truly effective and profound, it is essential that you carry out the 'attunement process' described below.

1. **Relax your body:** take several long deep breaths – concentrate on breathing out any tensions down through your body.

2. **Ground your energies:** focus on where your body is connecting with the chair you are sitting on and make sure that your feet are flat on the floor. Imagine that your whole body is getting heavier and that you are sinking deeper into the chair.

3. **Link to your source of inspiration:** imagine that you are now being surrounded by a bright and beautiful light which is flowing around and through you – make sure this light travels all the way through your body into your feet and into the earth beneath you.

4. **Ask for guidance and protection:** connect to the Universal Healing Vibration by silently, in your own words, saying:

'I ask the Divine Creator that I may only receive the healing which is for my Highest Good at this point in time. I ask that I receive healing only from the highest and purest light frequencies. May my healing process be watched over and guided by the angelic. May the healing light connect with every aspect of my being in a way that is in accordance with the Divine Will and my own soul purpose in this life, at this time.'

CHOOSING AND CASTING THE CRYSTALS
1. Position the Healing Wheel directly in front of you. Take a few deep breaths and try to still your mind, then clearly focus and concentrate on the following question, 'What healing

> Important Note: *Before you start, it is important to cleanse your crystals as detailed on pages 12–13. This is to ensure that the healing you receive is safe and for your Highest Good.*

qualities do I need at this time?' As you think this question, choose three to five crystals from the pouch – no more than five should be chosen at this stage, often three is sufficient – do not feel you have to choose more than three.

2. Look at the crystals you have chosen. Identify them and make a mental note about the impression you have from these crystals. You can, if you wish, read about each of the crystals now or do this later after you have cast them.

3. Now clearly focus on the question, 'Where do I need these healing qualities in my energy system at this time?' Then, holding the crystals between the palms of your hands 5–8 centimetres (2–3 inches) above the centre of the wheel, let them drop onto the Healing Wheel.

Important Notes:

• *Sometimes a crystal will seem to 'span' more than one sphere. Usually it will seem more comfortable in one than the other, in which case move it into the centre of that sphere. Occasionally you may prefer to leave the crystal 'aspecting' both spheres, in which case the crystal will be healing both areas indicated.*

• *Ignore any crystals which have fallen beyond the spheres – these can be put to one side or replaced in the pouch.*

• *Very rarely, all the crystals will fall outside the Healing Wheel. If this happens, replace all crystals in the pouch and repeat the process, paying particular attention to your preparation, and making sure that you are clearly focusing, both when you select the crystals and when you cast them onto the wheel. If again all the crystals fall beyond the wheel this is a sign that it is not appropriate for you to receive crystal healing with the wheel on this occasion and you should not try to work with the Healing Wheel until the following day.*

---

4. Identify which spheres have been 'aspected' by the crystals.

RECEIVING THE HEALING

The simplest and most effective method is to focus on the thought, 'I am open to receive the healing which is for my Highest Good and most appropriate for me at this time.'

Allow your eyes to notice the patterns which are formed with the crystals and the symbols on the Healing Wheel. Then close your eyes and try to recall the pattern with your inner eye. Finally, imagine rays of light radiating from this pattern towards you and ask that these healing frequencies heal and balance your energy field. You may wish to imagine that you are breathing in the essence of the crystals and the symbols.

Take a few moments to relax and enjoy the feeling of your whole energy system being lovingly balanced and healed. If you are very sensitive, you may even feel tingling sensations in different parts of your body.

After a few moments you may find it of interest to refer to the various spheres and crystals, to see which parts of your energy field are being healed and balanced at this time and the particular healing vibration your chosen crystals are radiating. This may help you to understand your energy system more. Also, each sphere section contains ideas and other suggested therapies that can help to balance that aspect of your being. Whilst reading about the crystals and spheres you may like to leave the crystals in place on the wheel so that the healing continues.

Important Note: *The healing process takes place without understanding or reading the significance of the symbols and crystals.*

If you wish to really feel and understand a particular sphere, take the crystal from the wheel and place it on the symbol on the relevant page in this book so it emphasizes that aspect for you.

You can leave the crystals in place on the Healing Wheel for just a few minutes or much longer if you so wish. However, ensure the wheel is not disturbed and that you can quickly remove a crystal if the healing sensations become too intense. Some healers like to leave the crystals in place overnight or whilst they meditate. It is just a question of personal preference – find out what works best for you.

> Important Note: *You will receive much more benefit from your healing if you are able to rest for a few hours afterwards followed by a good night's sleep. It is recommended that you drink several glasses of mineral water and avoid heavy foods and alcohol. Your energy system will then be able to assimilate the finer crystal healing frequencies more effectively. You may be aware of the healing process taking place over several days. It is usually recommended not to repeat the healing process until at least three days have elapsed – an interval of one week suits most people.*

COMPLETING THE HEALING

Carefully remove the crystals from the wheel. Cleanse them prior to placing them back in their pouch *(see pages 12–13 for details)*. Either cleanse them straight away or set them aside until later when you have more time. Do not use the crystals again for readings or healings until you have cleansed them. It is possible for crystals to absorb vibrations that have been discarded during the healing process and these would not be helpful in further readings and healings.

Focus on breathing in and at the same time feeling your physical body connecting to the chair and floor.

If you wish, make a note of the crystals selected and the spheres that were aspected.

Put the wheels away. As you return them to the box, affirm that you are also 'closing down' *(see page 105)* your intuitive gifts at this time.

Stand up and have a good stretch, rub your hands together firmly in order to ensure you are well grounded.

Blow out the candle, and at the same time send out a thought of love and thanks for the healing you have just received.

HEALING OTHERS WITH THE HEALING WHEEL

Virtually the same process applies as when you heal yourself except for the following points.

Align the Healing Wheel directly in front of your client who should be sitting opposite you – you will see the spheres upside down. Now guide your client through the process, following the guidelines described earlier, including the request for protection and healing. Please read Using Crystals for Healing *(see pages 100–105)* before healing others with the Healing Wheel.

> Important Note: *This type of healing is potentially very powerful – please only give healing to those who truly want it. Healing should never be given without the full permission of the client – however well meaning the intentions of the healer.*

OTHER WAYS OF USING THE HEALING WHEEL

INTUITIVE HEALING
Spread all twelve crystals in front of you, not on the Healing Wheel. Now select as many or as few as you wish, depending on which attract you, and place these wherever you feel inspired onto the wheel. Try to do this reflectively, without preconceived ideas of geometric patterns. Try to feel where each crystal belongs. When the pattern has formed, simply sit in front of it for a few moments and follow the instructions for receiving healing. This is more effective with people who know little or nothing about the crystals and who do not know what the symbols represent.

HEALING A RELATIONSHIP
The Healing Wheel can be adapted to heal a rift between two people – providing both are present and equally desirous of healing the rift. Each person chooses two crystals. The crystals are cast in turn until all four are on the wheel. The heal-ing proceeds as usual but relates to the energy fields of both participants when together. Our subtle energy systems can change dramatically when in the presence of people with whom we have a relationship. This is why it is essential that both participants do the exercise together. This healing process can help you see and understand those changes and interactions of the energy field.

PROFESSIONAL HEALING THERAPY
Experienced therapists can use the Healing Wheel in their professional practice. Ask your patients to choose the crystals and cast them in the usual way with eyes closed, focusing on where they need healing qualities, or suggest they select the spheres and crystals to create a unique mandala that 'feels right' for them. The patterns formed with either method can be very revealing and give you insight into the type of healing required by the patient at that time.

The Chakras

| Base | Sacral | Solar Plexus | Heart | Throat | Brow | Crown |

Traditionally, it is considered that there are seven major chakras, or energy centres as they are sometimes referred to, in the human energy system, each relating to parts of the body, organs and glands. Each chakra is associated with different functions and correlates to a spectrum colour and one of the five senses. In addition, they each relate to one of the seven levels of the aura, sometimes known as the subtle bodies.

The word 'chakra' derives from the Sanskrit word for 'wheel'. Psychic perception is a very personal thing, but most clairvoyants agree that the analogy of a wheel of energy is an accurate description of a chakra. Chakras are also often symbolized as flowers opening – for example, the thousand-petalled lotus is a favoured description for the Crown Chakra at the top of the head. They are also perceived to be like cones or cups and the symbolism of a chalice is often used for the Crown Chakra.

CHAKRAS AS ENERGY CENTRES

Chakras are points of concentrated energy which help us to accept, assimilate and give out life force or energy. They are sometimes described as energy transformers, which monitor the amount of energy entering and leaving the energy field. Depending on circumstances and the state of the energy field, chakras can seem lethargic and slow moving or sparky and over-active. Ideally, each chakra will be balanced with its six counterparts, so energy works evenly throughout the system. However, a perfectly balanced and harmonious chakra system is relatively rare and a degree of imbalance is essential to allow changes and spiritual evolution to take place. Therefore such imbalances should be viewed as signs of positive growth and not a cause for worry or alarm.

Crystals on the chakra spheres can help in many different ways. They may encourage the chakra to be more open and receptive to the vital life-force energy which is continuously available within the Universe, thus speeding up the chakra's ability to assimilate energies. They can also help the chakra to strengthen its linking structure, so it connects and transports energy between the physical and spiritual dimensions more effectively. In addition, they may support and gently slow down an over-extended highly sensitive chakra which is making a spiritual shift, thus helping it to make the transition from slower moving energies to higher frequencies at a more comfortable and steady pace.

Look at the quality of the crystal which has been cast onto the chakra sphere. This may help you to understand the type of imbalance that has occurred within the energy centre. It can indicate that the chakra may need to be opened and expanded or closed and contracted. It may need to be strengthened and protected or

71

THE SEVEN CHAKRAS AND SEVEN LEVELS OF THE AURA

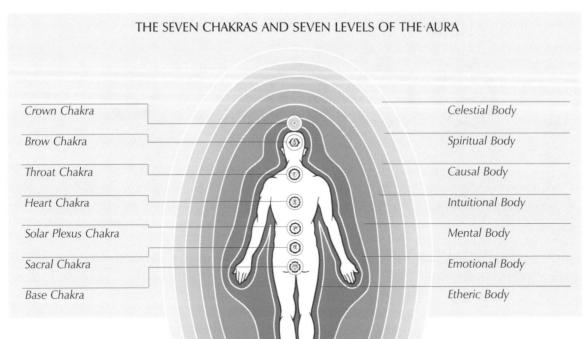

Crown Chakra	Celestial Body
Brow Chakra	Spiritual Body
Throat Chakra	Causal Body
Heart Chakra	Intuitional Body
Solar Plexus Chakra	Mental Body
Sacral Chakra	Emotional Body
Base Chakra	Etheric Body

cleared of congestion and old energy patterns.

To balance the chakra, you can leave the crystal in its position on the Healing Wheel – the healing will automatically start to be transferred to the chakra. If you wish to become more actively involved in the healing process, you may like to take the crystal and hold it in your hand or hold it to the centre of the chakra. You may wish to visualize the spectrum colour that is indicated for that chakra (see below), wear this colour or choose a crystal from your kit which matches the colour. Included in the section on each chakra are further ideas suggesting how to balance and heal that aspect of the energy field (see pages 74–80).

THE SEVEN CHAKRAS
The Base Chakra, also known as the root chakra and 'muladhara' in Sanskrit, is located at the coccyx – the base of the spine – or, according to some authorities, at the perineum. The spectrum colour attributed to this chakra is red and it governs the sense of smell.

The Sacral Chakra, or 'svadisthana', is also called the spleen or splenic chakra. This is a little misleading as it is positioned approximately 5–10 centimetres (2–4 inches) below the

Important Note: *The traditional correspondences of glands and functions vary slightly between different systems and philosophies. The notes given here are for guidance only. If you wish to find out more about one of the chakras, particularly if they are regularly aspected for you in the Healing Wheel, please study this fascinating subject in greater depth – there are many excellent books on the subject (see Bibliography and Further Reading, page 111).*

naval. It is also sometimes referred to as the 'hara' and is considered a centre of power and balance in Japanese and Chinese martial arts. The Sacral Chakra's spectrum colour is orange and it governs the sense of taste.

In Sanskrit, the Solar Plexus Chakra is known as 'manipura'. It is located in the upper stomach, approximately 10 centimetres (4 inches) below the tip of the sternum. The spectrum colour attributed to this chakra is yellow, which can evolve into a spectacular gold. Some systems attribute the sense of smell to the Solar Plexus Chakra and others the sense of sight.

The Heart Chakra, or 'anahata', is found in the centre of the chest area in line with the physical heart. Its spectrum colour is green, but it is also often associated with pink or a combination of these two colours. The Heart Chakra governs the sense of touch.

The Throat Chakra, known as 'visuddha', is situated in the neck, near the Adam's apple and over the larynx and thyroid gland. The spectrum colour of the Throat Chakra is pale to mid blue, although turquoise is also often associated with this energy centre. It governs the sense of hearing.

Often referred to as the 'third eye' or 'ajna', in Sanskrit, the Brow Chakra is located in the middle of the forehead at a point roughly in line with the bridge of the nose, however, its position does vary from one individual to another. The Brow Chakra's spectrum colour is indigo blue. There are some healers who associate it with violet – the traditional colour for the Crown Chakra – they feel pure white or clear light should be attributed to the Crown. The 'sixth' sense is aptly associated with the Brow Chakra which rules visualization, imagination and clairvoyance.

Known as the 'sahasrara' or 'lotus of a thousand petals', the Crown Chakra is located at the top of the head, or at a point just above this.

Some teach that its position correlates to the fontanelle or 'soft spot' found in the skull and is the physical entry and exit point for the spirit. The spectrum colour usually attributed to the Crown Chakra is violet, or sometimes pure gold, symbolizing wisdom of the gods. Also it is often said to resonate with white light, which contains all the colours of the spectrum.

SYMBOLISM

In the Healing Wheel, the chakras have been represented using a simplified version of the Hindu symbology. The Base Chakra is depicted as a lotus of four petals within which is a square, a traditional symbol of earth, and a downward-pointing triangle. The Sacral Chakra has a lotus of six petals, containing a crescent moon, which is a classic symbol of femininity, nurturance and fertility. The Solar Plexus Chakra has a lotus of ten petals and a downward-pointing triangle. The Heart Chakra is depicted with a lotus of twelve petals and two intersecting triangles which form six points, giving the impression of a star radiating in all directions. The Throat Chakra has a sixteen-petalled lotus containing a downward-pointing triangle which, in turn, contains a smaller circle, said to symbolize the manifestation of speech. The Brow Chakra, also known as the third eye, is interestingly symbolized with only two petals of the lotus. There are many interpretations for this: some say this relates to the wings required to fly up to spirit; others feel it represents the two physical eyes. This lotus contains a downward-pointing triangle. The seventh chakra, the Crown Chakra, is often referred to as the 'thousand-petalled lotus' – the number one thousand is thought to represent the infinite and the Crown Chakra is without limit – it is therefore aptly symbolized with the impression of a lotus with an infinite number of petals.

The Base Chakra

The Base Chakra rules the physical body, manifestation and the ability to ground the energy field. It is the source of your survival instinct and life force. The root of your individuality, stability and point of inner stillness is anchored here. The way you function in the physical world depends on the state of your Base Chakra.

The Base Chakra stores the vital life force from which you derive the will to live. It is a starting point in the energy field and can register the shock of birth, feelings of loneliness and stress. It rules the adrenal glands, feet, legs, bones and large intestine and governs the ability to manifest thoughts, ideas and feelings.

The Base Chakra is associated with the Mineral Realm and Element of Earth. If it dysfunctions, you may find your ability to operate in the physical world is impaired. You could be overly attached to physical matters and place great importance on possessions and material success. This can lead to difficulty in letting go in order to move on to new areas – making changes could be challenging. Alternatively, you may become extremely sensitive and find daily life is almost painfully unbearable.

Feelings of being 'spaced out' and disorientated can occur when the Base Chakra is insufficiently open and clear in order to anchor the energy system onto the Earth. Physical symptoms can include eating disorders, constipation, sciatica and problems with the feet, legs and lower back. If you are lacking in energy and vitality, feel uncomfortable on the earth plane or 'earthbound', look for imbalances in this chakra.

To heal and balance the Base Chakra, look at ways to strengthen your connection to the Earth: walking in the countryside is often a good idea and you may find it helpful to receive reflexology treatments. Physical exercise such as tai chi, dance and movement can be useful. Make time in your life for practical and mundane tasks: the routine and familiarity of physical chores is a useful earthing technique.

SURVIVAL • GROUNDING • MANIFESTATION

The Sacral Chakra

The Sacral Chakra rules the emotions, assimilation and sexual energy. It is the centre of femininity and balance, and is also a centre of desire, which can motivate you or overwhelm you. Your gut reactions and emotional responses to the world are ruled by the state of your Sacral Chakra.

The Sacral Chakra is concerned with the fluids of the body and therefore governs circulation and urinary elimination. It also rules the ovaries and testes, sexuality and reproduction. Some systems teach that it is the Base Chakra which rules the sexual and reproductive energies and there is still discussion and debate over this.

The Sacral Chakra is associated with the Plant Realm and the Element of Water. If it dysfunctions, you may experience digestive problems and feel powerless. There may be illness related to the bladder, kidneys and sexual organs. Extreme desires and cravings can be felt if the Sacral Chakra is out of balance.

Feelings of being overwhelmed with emotion or an inability to absorb and process all that is around you can indicate that the Sacral Chakra is overloaded. It may need to contract slightly and be strengthened. If it has become tight and inflexible, you may have difficulty registering feelings or digesting and absorbing vital life-force energy from the foods you eat. Sexual problems will also register in the Sacral Chakra. When it is functioning in a balanced state it will help lead you from separation into a state of unity.

To heal and balance this centre, look at how to improve your ability to assimilate and digest all that comes to you. This may involve dietary changes or training yourself to respond differently to life experiences and challenges. You might need to teach yourself to cope more effectively with stress. Drink plenty of mineral water and become aware of the healing powers of purification. Look for safe ways of first acknowledging and then releasing your negative feelings and fears.

ASSIMILATION • SEXUALITY • EMOTIONS

The Solar Plexus Chakra

The Solar Plexus Chakra rules the mental and intellectual aspects of the energy field. When this chakra is strong and balanced you will feel centred and secure with a clear sense of identity. This centre is the source of your personal power and can guide you towards self-mastery.

The Solar Plexus Chakra rules the pancreas, the metabolism and the mental regulation of emotional processes. It is more often here that we feel 'heartache' as this is where we usually connect to others in relationships and feel the pain of separation when the relationship is over.

The Solar Plexus Chakra is associated with the Animal Realm and the Element of Air, with a secondary association to Fire. If it dysfunctions, you may experience physical problems such as stomach ulcers, diabetes, nervous disorders and exhaustion. At a non-physical level, you may lose your sense of identity or develop an over-inflated ego and sense of self-importance.

Feelings of vulnerability occur when the Solar Plexus needs healing. You may also lack humour, will-power and a sense of perspective when facing challenges. Addictive behaviour can stem from a weakness of this centre, leading to a dependence on drugs or alcohol and obsessive behaviour. If this chakra is temporarily over-sensitized, unreleased anger can explode when unexpectedly triggered. Aspire to being true to yourself and not living up to an image demanded from you by others. The Solar Plexus can be a source of courage and power when in balance.

To heal and balance this chakra, find ways of bringing laughter and joy into your life. Try therapies such as assertiveness training and group work that help you develop self-worth and self-esteem, whilst also considering the feelings and needs of others. Find safe ways to release feelings of frustration, anger and resentment. Deep breathing into the diaphragm can calm and soothe this centre. Use aromatherapy oils and massage to warm and soothe the chakra.

POWER ● WILL ● EGO

The Heart Chakra

The Heart Chakra is positioned at the halfway point in the chakra system. It represents the point of balance and the gateway between the physical and non-physical worlds. Through compassion and absolute love, it is possible to access the spiritual vibrations on the dense earthly plane.

It is through the Heart Chakra that we express compassion, find equilibrium and know our connection with other realms, life forms and fellow humans. It is said that the Heart Chakra is the last centre to truly open and is the point from which healers radiate the healing frequency. To have a truly open heart centre is to become one with all that exists and brings about a state of spiritual ecstasy.

The Heart Chakra is associated with the Human Realm and the Element of Fire, with a secondary association to the Element of Air. It rules the thymus gland, lungs, arms and hands as well as the heart, circulation and blood. If it dysfunctions, there may be breathing problems, such as asthma and bronchitis, lung and heart disease, high blood pressure and strokes. Feelings of being overstretched and under extreme pressure can show up in the Heart Chakra, which often acts as a safety valve, exploding when there is too much energy in the system with no effective outlet.

Imbalances in the Heart Chakra can result in imbalances in giving and receiving. If you do not value yourself, you may end up giving far more than you allow yourself to receive, and as a result your energy reserves become severely depleted.

To heal the Heart Chakra find relaxation techniques that work well for you. Yoga exercises, which involve stretching out the spine, chest area and arms, and deep-breathing exercises may be helpful. Explore ways of forgiving yourself and others for past mistakes. Try to understand when you or others act from a point of vulnerability, then feel compassion. Practise unconditional sharing, giving and receiving.

UNCONDITIONAL LOVE ● UNITY ● COMPASSION

The Throat Chakra

This chakra moves away from the material plane and introduces the energy system to the celestial dimension of light. From this centre comes the ability to trust that the universe will provide sustenance at all levels. Your Throat Chakra will help you to recognize spiritual truth and your part in the cosmic plan.

The Throat Chakra rules communication at many levels, including speech, hearing (celestial sounds as well as earthly ones), symbolism and telepathy. It rules the thyroid and parathyroid glands, the neck and shoulder areas and governs the ability to express, communicate and be creative. When balanced, it gives insight into the more spiritual realms of existence.

The Throat Chakra is associated with the Planetary Realm and the Element of Ether. Sore throats, feeling choked and creative blocks can all be caused by a dysfunctional Throat Chakra. Similarly, stiff necks, frozen shoulders and problems with the thyroid, hearing and ears could be signs of a blockage in this centre.

Over-sympathizing with others may indicate a need to develop detachment which can come from the throat area. Loss of sensitivity to tone and speech difficulties can also occur when the Throat Chakra is blocked. This area can house deep-rooted fears of not being good enough and an unwillingness to take full responsibility for one's own existence, a duty synonymous with spiritual maturity. If you are unable to see the beauty in life or to be inspired and receive ideas, this chakra may need healing.

To heal and balance the Throat Chakra, find different ways of expressing yourself. You may need to ask if you are speaking your truth and being heard. Art therapy may give you the creative release and outlet that can help to dispel whatever is blocking the throat. Sound therapy could also be effective, whether it is chanting or singing, or simply listening to music that inspires you. Ensure your life is a true expression of your spiritual self.

COMMUNICATION • CREATIVITY • INSIGHT

The Brow Chakra

The Brow Chakra is considered to be the seat of wisdom and keeper of the soul memory. It is the centre of vision, intuition and spiritual perception. Your Brow Chakra will help you to see and understand at a universal level. From this point, you can develop discernment and the ability to create matter from thought.

The Brow Chakra is said to be the final doorway through which one passes before entering the oneness of the Universe, where we relinquish all sense of individuality. From this chakra comes your appreciation of light, colour and beautiful images. It is the seat of your intuition and is said to hold the record of all your past lives, so flashes of distant memory may occur when this centre is activated.

The Brow Chakra is associated with the Angelic Realm. It rules the pituitary gland and the autonomic nervous system. Some teachings associate the pineal gland with the Brow Chakra and the pituitary gland with the Crown Chakra.

If you are feeling disorientated and confused, the Brow Chakra may be out of balance. If this chakra is dysfunctioning, vision problems may occur: in the physical sense, these may take the form of blindness, eye strain and blurred vision; in the esoteric sense, delusions and hallucinations can occur. There may also be problems with headaches and other eye problems. It is through this centre that the soul impulse is registered and that you can see your soul path and make a commitment to a life of service. If you feel spiritually directionless, you may wish to heal the Brow Chakra.

To heal this centre, it is important to find the appropriate method of meditation. However, regular meditators may need to stop for a while as it is possible to overstretch the Brow Chakra. If you have not practised meditation before, it is better to start with simple methods and only for short periods of time (*see Chapter Five for explanation*). It is not advisable to place a crystal on the forehead as the brow centre is especially sensitive.

VISION ● IMAGINATION ● INTUITION

The Crown Chakra

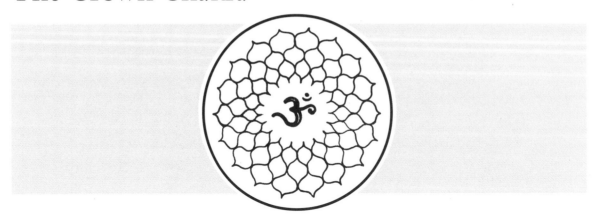

The Crown Chakra is the Divine connection, linking the physical to the celestial. It is the entry point for celestial wisdom and inspiration, and the point of integration which brings coherence to the whole energy system. It is the centre of limitless possibilities and infinite opportunities for spiritual growth.

Through your Crown Chakra, you can receive spiritual guidance and understanding, which you can then choose whether or not to accept. If this centre is open and strong, you will have a clear link to the celestial realms, feel guided and supported and able to draw upon spiritual values in your daily life.

The Crown Chakra is associated with the 'All That Is' sphere and the Angelic Realm. It is usually said to rule the pineal gland, although some say it rules the pituitary gland. Until recently, it was thought that the pineal gland had no function at all; it is now believed to rule moods, brain chemistry and is highly sensitive to light.

Feelings of alienation, depression and confusion can occur if the Crown Chakra is out of balance. You can feel cut off from your source of Divine inspiration, unable to comprehend the patterns that run through your life. You may be confused by spiritual matters. This chakra is often symbolized by the chalice – it is there waiting for you to acknowledge its presence and reactivate when you are ready. The link with the Divine can only ever be perfect – rarely is it damaged. However, this link may need to be consciously acknowledged and accepted in your life.

To heal and balance the Crown Chakra, look at ways of introducing meditation practices into your life. Or if a regular meditator, you may need to review your practice. Seek out sacred places or find time for a spiritual retreat. This will help you renew and strengthen your link to the Divine. Seek experiences which help you to transcend. Allow a transformational shift to take place within you. Find groups which support you to retrieve your spark of original creativity.

TRANSCENDENCE • MEDITATION • ENLIGHTENMENT

The Realms of Consciousness

Mineral

Plant

Animal

Human

Planetary

Angelic

The realms of consciousness relate to the different planes of existence. In order to interact completely and holistically with the Cosmos and integrate life's experiences, we need to feel at ease in each one of these different worlds. However, it is usual to feel far more comfortable and at home in some realms than in others. Ideally, you will happily translate from one plane of existence into another with complete ease. The aim is to feel equally at ease in any part of the Universe! Can you communicate equally well with the rocks and trees, the planets and the angels, and also your fellow humans?

If you tend to function well in only some of the realms, these areas can become overstretched. Ideally, you want to spread the energetic burden and relate equally well to all the dimensions making up the Universe. Also, at times, we need to strengthen our link with the realms in order to deepen our understanding of the other levels of existence. Crystals aspecting one of the realms will indicate the need to rebalance your connection to that plane of existence.

THE SIX REALMS OF THE HEALING WHEEL

There are six realms of consciousness represented in the Healing Wheel. The Mineral Realm deals with manifestation and action. The Plant Realm relates to the world of thoughts and feelings. The Animal Realm rules our instinct and intuitive responses to the world. The Human Realm rules our ability to relate with our fellow man and have a sense of brotherhood and sisterhood. The Planetary Realm makes us aware of the small but vital part we play within the greater whole. And, finally, the Angelic Realm reminds us of the vast spiritual dimensions which surround our existence.

REALMS AS LIFE PATTERNS

The realms all hold memories of past existences, deep-rooted emotions and fears as well as memories of previous experiences – these may need to be exorcized from your soul. They will also hold lessons, challenges and records of unfinished business. Explore the various realms to discover where you feel safe and familiar. Notice if you have a greater rapport with some realms more than others. You may dislike one realm or feel uncomfortable within it. The realm you most resist can, in time, become your greatest ally. Subconsciously you probably know that within this realm there are many challenges, lessons and unresolved issues!

You may also be too immersed in one realm, to the detriment of the others. For example, many people need to heal their connection to the Human Realm – they often feel more at ease with plants, animals or the angels. Healing the Human Realm can help them to come to terms with their own sense of being and relate better to other humans.

REALMS WITHIN THE AURA

Each of the realms of consciousness has an affinity with one of the levels of the aura *(see diagram on page 72)*.

The Mineral Realm relates to the first level of the aura, usually called the etheric body, which is the subtle body most closely linked with the physical body – here patterns of potential diseases and imbalances can first register before actually manifesting in the physical body. It is essential that this part of the energy system is kept healthy and full of vital life-force.

The Plant Realm connects to the second level of the aura known as the emotional body, sometimes referred to as the astral body. This level of the aura is quite fluid and flexible. It does not echo the physical body in the same way as the etheric but it is still relatively dense and can hold emotions within it. If emotional patterns become stuck and stagnant within this field it is possible for disease to manifest.

The Animal Realm relates to the third level of the aura, usually called the mental body. However, this title can be confusing as it relates to instinctive thoughts more than the intellect.

The Human Realm is linked to the fourth level of the aura, sometimes called the intuitional body. This point within the subtle energy system is often considered the interface between the physical and spiritual realms.

The Planetary Realm is associated with the fifth level of the aura, often called the causal body – also referred to as the 'template'. This level is thought to contain the 'blueprint' for the soul's incarnation. Potential for learning and major life lessons may be stored here – these will be triggered and release their message at crucial points during the soul's lifetime.

Finally, the Angelic Realm connects to the sixth level of the aura, sometimes called the spiritual body. This point acts as the final gateway between the individual soul vibration and the collective celestial frequencies.

ASSOCIATIONS AND CORRELATIONS

In the Healing Wheel, the realms are correlated to a chakra and an element as well as one of the subtle levels of the aura. Each realm is symbolized very simply with pictorial representations of its dimension.

The Mineral Realm has a seven-pointed quartz cluster with seven inner growth marks known as 'phantoms' within the central crystal. Crystals are considered the purest of all minerals and seven is a sacred number and also corresponds to the seven chakras. The Plant Realm shows the 'Cosmic Tree' which has two branches from one central root source, symbolizing duality and unity, and the ancient Egyptian hieroglyphic of the papyrus dating back to 3000 BC. The Animal Realm represents a spectrum of creatures: the eagle symbolizes winged creatures and transcendence; the lion, traditionally the ruler, represents land-based animals in the realm; the serpent, symbol of transformation and power, denotes the reptiles; and the dolphin, a much loved and revered creature, represents the animals who live in the sea. The Human Realm shows the image of the universal man connecting into the universal web of consciousness symbolizing the interconnectedness of the whole. The orbiting planets, representing the Planetary Realm, remind us that Earth is just one part of a greater picture. Finally, the angel surrounded by points of light reminds us of the spiritual dimension upon which we can call.

The Mineral Realm

The Mineral Realm rules the physical dimension. It relates to the base upon which you build your life and all the structures within it. This realm is the starting point and foundation of all creative forces within the realms. All that you can see and touch, which has shape and form, is encompassed within the Mineral Realm.

In this realm you can discover more about your relationship to the Earth and all physical aspects of life. Learn how to feel safe and secure in your body and on this planet. Discover the potential strengths of your physical being. Rocks, stones and crystals are the building blocks of the planet and microcosmic particles of these same minerals are found in the human body, forming intricate patterns of sacred geometry.

The Mineral Realm is associated with the Base Chakra and Element of Earth. Crystals cast onto this sphere can indicate that you need to focus on your physical body. It may be that your whole body is being rejuvenated, or you are reminded to adopt a more balanced lifestyle – avoid stress or overexertion.

If you feel uncomfortable within this realm, you may want to avoid the mundane aspects of life or find practical skills extremely challenging and unfulfilling. Your body loses its flexibility – as if a crystallization process is taking over – stiff joints, arthritic conditions and aches and pains can occur. Your body may be deficient in vital minerals and could seem to be weaker and more fragile than normal.

To strengthen your connection with the Mineral Realm, look at the therapies recommended for the Base Chakra and Element of Earth. Walking barefoot on sand can be very helpful. Exercise to strengthen the body and use movement to improve its flow of energy – tai chi or yoga may be particularly beneficial. Work on the bones and structure of your body and consider therapies such as cranial sacral osteopathy. You may respond to taking tissues salts and mineral supplements.

THE WORLD OF MANIFESTATION AND ACTION

The Plant Realm

The Plant Realm rules your ability to feel and instinctively know what is happening around you. It governs your interaction with your environment and your emotional response to people and situations. It also helps you to accept the different phases of life and move on fluidly.

In this realm you can learn to experience the full range of emotions from great joy to deep sadness, from anger to exhilaration, without holding on to the emotion once the moment has passed.

The Plant Realm correlates to the Sacral Chakra and the Element of Water. Your relationship with this realm will be reflected in the living and working environments you choose as well as your reactions to unseen but nonetheless very real feelings and instincts.

If the Plant Realm feels alien to you, it is possible that there are emotional issues in your life which need to be addressed. An inability to accept nourishment and sustenance literally from our diets and esoterically from life indicates a need to balance this realm. You may find yourself resisting changes and being unwilling to

move on to a new phase in your life when this realm is fragile. If you are unhappy with the atmosphere in your home or place of work, try to redress the balance so it feels more harmonious to you, possibly introducing plants and flowers into the space.

To strengthen your connection with the Plant Realm, you may wish to use herbal remedies which use plant extracts, flower and tree essences and aromatherapy oils. Look at your diet to ensure you are including enough fruit and vegetables. Hugging a tree really does work! A more conventional approach may be to do some gardening – try planting some shrubs, flowers or trees. Whilst walking in forests or meadows filled with plants, consciously try to breathe in the life-force radiated by the Plant Realm to nourish your being.

THE WORLD OF EMOTION AND FEELING

The Animal Realm

The Animal Realm rules the dimension of instinctive thought, governing your ability to face your deepest fears and accept your own power. Reserves of vitality, drive and your survival instinct all reside within this realm. Awaken the primal strength of your animal aspect to give you courage, guidance and protection.

In this realm you learn to harness the power of the animal which resides within you by taming it with love. Integrate and accept this instinctual aspect of yourself. In many cultures – Native American, for instance – animals are considered to be protectors and sacred guides.

The Animal Realm is associated with the Solar Plexus Chakra and Elements of Air and Fire. Genetically inherited patterns can be laid down within this realm – these may be helpful or hindering. First recognize them and then choose whether or not you wish to clear them from your energy field.

If you do not relate easily to the Animal Realm, you may find it difficult to act on your instincts. You may prefer to deliberate slowly and carefully before taking action, and tend to block the primal drives which lie within us all. Misuse of power and violent outbursts may arise due to blocks in this realm. An inability to control greed and lust can occur when this realm is out of balance. Parts of the psyche which are repressed, ignored or neglected may dramatically and suddenly raise issues in this realm.

A simple but effective method to strengthen your connection with the Animal Realm is to spend time with different animals and observe their natural instinctive patterns of behaviour. Try stroking a pet! Learn to respect animals and understand the wisdom that has evolved over time within different species. Work with animal cards and discover your totem animals. Distinguish your own patterns of behaviour from those you have inherited or adopted from others which are not helpful to you. Learn to respect animals as equals sharing the Universe with you.

THE WORLD OF INSTINCT AND THOUGHT

The Human Realm

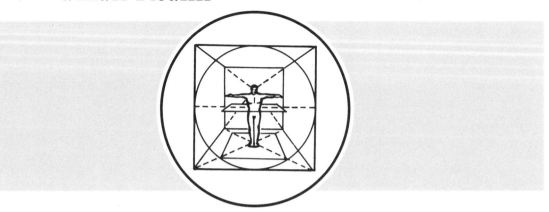

The Human Realm governs our connection to our fellow humans. When the link is strong and pure we are able to feel a sense of sisterhood and brotherhood. We are able to see beyond prejudices and differences in culture and feel part of one loving family.

It is in this realm that we discover how to love unconditionally, accept the vulnerability within both ourselves and others and learn forgiveness. Within this realm you can learn the art of loving detachment to help you serve the light more ably.

The Human Realm is associated with the Heart Chakra and Elements of Fire and Air. Through this realm we can experience unity; it may act as a doorway through which the spiritual worlds can greet the more physical realms. It is therefore important that this dimension is clear and freely flowing around you.

If you do not feel comfortable within the Human Realm, you may experience problems of self-esteem and find it hard to accept yourself as you are. You may constantly be striving to change your body image and personality, and may not have a clear sense of identity. You might also find it difficult to feel compassion for others, preferring to judge them. Or you may over-identify with them, feeling the pain, grief and suffering of the whole world and drowning in sorrow to a point where you cannot function.

To deepen your understanding and strengthen your link to the Human Realm, try to see the points of unity within yourself and humanity; look at what we all have in common. Reflect on the concept that what one human being experiences is felt at some subtle level by every other human on the planet; we therefore share experiences and, if united, have a wonderful opportunity to grow spiritually. Discover that as you give love freely to more and more beings you have yet more love to give. Experience the unifying feeling of loving unconditionally.

THE WORLD OF UNCONDITIONAL LOVE AND COMPASSION

The Planetary Realm

The Planetary Realm starts to link you to the world of the collective. It represents the greater whole of which you are just one part. This is the dimension where the soul plan is laid down. As you look beyond the personal into the collective, you may perceive your spiritual mission for this incarnation.

Let the Planetary Realm overawe you. Acknowledge the mystery of the great unknown and allow the enormity of the Universe to put your life back into perspective – see your part in the great whole. This realm rules global consciousness and the recognition of the part each living thing plays in the Universal Plan.

The Planetary Realm is associated with the Throat Chakra and the Element of Ether. It is in this realm that we learn to hear spiritual guidance and find our place within the Universe. Your unique energy signature is laid down in this part of the energy field; and crystals aspecting this realm may activate pre-coded messages, reminding you of your mission on Earth.

If your connection with the Planetary Realm needs strengthening or reconnecting, you may feel lost and disorientated, with no sense of pur-pose to your life. If you cannot see the wisdom and continuity within life's universal patterns and continuous cycles, the Planetary Realm can help. You may feel self-centred and be unwilling to work in group situations and share with others if this realm is not in harmony. You may unwittingly be responding to ancient memories and past-life experiences which are no longer relevant in this life.

To strengthen your connection with the Planetary Realm, make time to reflect and meditate regularly in order to recognize your unique role within the Universal Plan. Learn to respect the other realms and understand why you have a greater rapport with some more than others. An astrological consultation could help deepen your understanding of the planetary influences as they activate parts of your life.

THE WORLD OF THE UNIVERSAL COLLECTIVE

The Angelic Realm

The Angelic Realm rules the spiritual dimension and your link with the Divine. Your ability to hear the Divine messengers and to acknowledge the presence of your celestial protectors is governed by your connection with this realm. Allow your Angelic guides to raise your spiritual sights and aspirations.

In this realm we learn that there is far more in our world than that which can be measured in physical terms. We discover spiritual values and learn the importance of nurturing the spiritual dimension within our lives. It is vital to have the spiritual perspective to balance the physical, mental and emotional levels of being.

The Angelic Realm is associated with the Crown Chakra and Brow Chakra. Within the Angelic Realm you can learn to listen to the Divine messages being sent to you. The angels are wonderful examples of beauty and goodness that lie within everything – let them inspire you.

If you are not at ease with the Angelic Realm, you may need to raise your energetic frequency and connect to a more spiritual perspective in life. Alternatively, you may be over-sensitive to coarse vibrations at this time – protect yourself

until you can find time and space to explore this sensitivity. You may need to increase your ability to trust. Restore the innocence and wonder of childhood. Deepen your capacity for forgiveness.

To strengthen your connection with the Angelic Realm, look at the functions of angels and try to emulate them – discover how you can become a Divine messenger, light carrier and bearer of compassion to others. Can you become an angel on earth? Try working with angel cards and choose a card each day. Go to sacred spaces, perhaps on retreat, and ensure the place is 'holy' in your sense of the word. Remember it is essential that you ask for healing in order to start your process. Consult only therapists whom you intuitively feel work at the highest and purest vibrationary level – the therapist is more important than the therapy!

THE WORLD OF DIVINE SPIRIT

The Elements

Earth

Water

Air

Fire

Ether

The elements are the substances of which our beings are composed. They are the basic building blocks and fundamental energies of the Universe. Western tradition refers to the four elements of earth, water, air and fire, plus the element of ether, from which the other four originate. All five elements are present in every energy system, but the proportions and ways they manifest vary greatly in different individuals.

In Tibet, structures known as 'stupas' exist. They are made up of a large cube at the base, representing earth; resting upon this is a sphere to signify water; then a spiral-like structure to represent fire; and at the top is a crescent or half-moon shape to symbolize air, in which rests a small sphere denoting ether, which is the Tibetan word for the primary force from which the other elements flow.

Western astrology uses four elements to group the twelve signs of the zodiac. Aries, Leo and Sagittarius are the 'fire' signs. The 'earth' signs are Taurus, Virgo and Capricorn. Cancer, Scorpio and Pisces are ruled by 'water'. Gemini, Libra and Aquarius are the 'air' signs.

Chinese tradition talks of five elements (fire, earth, water, metal and wood). In various forms the elements are symbolized in every culture.

THE FIVE ELEMENTS OF THE HEALING WHEEL

Elements can give us strength, support and understanding of situations. If a crystal aspects an element in the Healing Wheel, discover how you can harness its power and healing qualities to help you. It is important to ensure the element is balanced within you. Earth contains energy and gives support, however it can also bury and become too solid. Water sustains and dispenses energy, it washes and cleanses but can also drown. Air stimulates the system helping you to breathe, yet it can also suffocate. Fire warms and energizes, but can also burn out. Ether has the ability to make an integrated whole and composite of all the other elements or it can lead to disintegration and random chaos.

Most people are a mixture of the elements, and in different situations, with different people and in various phases of life, the different element characteristics will be exhibited. It is interesting to observe in yourself and others when an element is becoming typified in your behaviour and personality. You may find that you resonate more easily with some elements than others.

Fiery types are considered dynamic but impatient. They love to start projects and at the outset are filled with enthusiasm and great vision. However, they may rush into something without necessarily thinking the whole matter through.

Earthy people bring practicality to a situation, they build and provide for themselves and those around them. They need security and stability, they make wonderful friends but can be just a little too dull and convention-bound at times.

Watery beings vacillate in the same way that the tides ebb and flow in response to the moon's phases. They unconditionally nurture and support others and often have wonderful artistic gifts. They are extremely sensitive to feelings – their own and those of others – this can lead to mood swings and unreliability or great insight and intuition.

The air types naturally think and observe, they value thoughts over feelings; intuition and compassion may present a mental dilemma for air.

Truly ethereal beings are rare. They seem to be living in two worlds at the same time; they have angelic qualities and yet live in the mundane world, they act as points of inspiration to all those whose lives they touch. They are often considered to be dreamy and slightly out of touch with day-to-day realities, but perhaps they simply live their lives by a different set of principles.

It is an empowering and useful strategy to recognize your element profile and consciously draw upon the strengths of the element you need for particular situations and challenges. If you wish to start a new project and you need courage, then draw upon the Element of Fire. When this project needs to be built with attention to detail and plans followed through to the end, draw upon the Element of Earth. To introduce artistic flair and intuitively respond to other people's needs, call upon the Element of Water. For objective reasoning draw upon the intellectual strengths of the Element of Air. Finally, draw in the Element of Ether to integrate the spiritual dimension into your project.

SOUL LESSONS

It is said that each element holds a lesson for the soul. The Element of Earth challenges you to manifest the Divine in your physical existence. Can you act out your spiritual principles in day-to-day life? The soul lesson of the Element of

Water is to learn how to become still and peaceful. Can you maintain a calm, smooth, watery surface to become a source of comfort and inspiration to others? The Element of Air challenges you to learn to control the mind. Can you discern between the intellectual human mind and wisdom of the Divine mind? The soul lesson of the Element of Fire is to learn about love. Can you discover how powerful the creative process can be when guided with pure and absolute love? Ether challenges you to learn to live life on Earth in accordance with spiritual law. Can you honour the spiritual vibration and yet maintain a fully integrated physical existence on Earth?

SYMBOLISM

In the Healing Wheel, the Elements of Earth, Water, Fire and Air have been represented using several traditional Western symbols. The four symbols representing the four suits in the tarot have been used: pentacle for Earth, chalice or cup for Water, sword for Air and wand for Fire. Also, ornamental symbols showing the movement or flow of the element have been incorporated into each sphere: the structured right-angled movement of Earth contrasts with the swirling waves of Water, and the undulating movement of Air contrasts with the fiery pointed direction of Fire. Two downward-pointing triangles represent Earth and Water, the two feminine elements, differentiated by the horizontal line crossing the Earth triangle. Two upward-pointing triangles represent the masculine Elements of Air and Fire. Air is differentiated also by a horizontal line crossing the triangle. These triangles are classical Western symbols for the elements. Ether is said to be the source of creation of the other four elements and is the void which becomes filled with spirit. Hence it is symbolized by seven open centres or vortices from which light is radiating out into the Universe.

The Element of Earth

The Element of Earth gives you strength both physically and mentally and governs your ability to be in touch with the reality of the day-to-day world. An inability to be grounded and cope with daily life on Earth or an overconcern with material matters are signs of the Earth element being out of balance.

If the Element of Earth is aspected with a crystal, it is a reminder to look at your relationship to the world. Look at your ability to be grounded and cope with mundane matters. Ensure you are not becoming buried and immersed by earthly desires, no longer able to see the wider picture.

The Element of Earth is associated with the Base Chakra and Mineral Realm. Check your physical body is in good health, particularly the structural support systems such as the bones and muscles. Devise a plan of action to restore your health – just thinking about doing it is not enough! Crystals cast onto the Element of Earth can strengthen you, help you act on your spiritual principles in earthly life and allow you to feel safe and secure on the planet.

When you need qualities such as endurance, passive strength, dependability, reliability and sheer hard-working perseverance, draw upon the strength of the Earth element. When it is balanced and working harmoniously within your system, you will find you have the gift of manifestation, which means things happen how and when you want them to.

To harness the healing qualities of Earth, look at practical activities which get your feet back on the ground and in touch with the Earth. Walking in nature, preferably barefoot on grass or sand, is very effective. Do some gardening; also mundane household chores can be very helpful. Include images of the Earth, such as plants, trees and grassy meadows, in your healing visualizations (*see Chapter Five*). Try physical therapies like massage, reflexology and shiatsu to help you get back in touch with your body.

PRACTICALITY ● STRENGTH ● ENDURANCE

The Element of Water

The Element of Water nourishes and sustains your being. It relates to the emotional aspects of your energy system, the part which senses and absorbs impressions of the world. If this area needs healing, you may feel oversensitive or swamped by other people's emotions.

If the Element of Water is aspected, you may need to become more sensitive towards others. As you develop this ability, you may detect the more subtle vibrations around you – even sensing companions' unspoken thoughts and feelings.

Water is associated with feeling and sensation, usually linked to the Sacral Chakra and Plant Realm. It rules the fluid content of the body, the bloodstream and glandular secretions. Oversensitivity may cause you to lose touch with your boundaries and your sense of identity. Crystals cast onto the Element of Water can help to calm and soothe you, so you become a source of comfort and inspiration to others.

If you feel it is an appropriate time to clear away old fears, grief and pain, then look at the Element of Water within your energy system.

Emotions which are no longer positively supporting you could be held here; cleanse them to make a fresh start. As this part of you comes into balance, you can assimilate feelings more effectively and get in touch with the real issues beyond what is happening on the surface.

To harness the healing qualities of Water, drink plenty of mineral water and go swimming. While bathing, affirm you will be physically and spiritually cleansed. Visualize yourself standing beneath a purifying waterfall or swimming in a pool of light. The moon, with its cyclic effect on the Earth's tides, is associated with the Element of Water. Monitor your personal response to the lunar cycle via your dreams and meditation. Use water-based flower and gem essences. Find a way of expressing and releasing emotions, possibly through some form of counselling.

EMOTIONS ● SUSTENANCE ● SENSITIVITY

The Element of Air

The Element of Air rules the power of thought and stimulates mental processes. The way you think and the ideas you formulate are governed by your connection with the Air. Unrealistic ideas and overemphasis of the intellect can indicate a need to balance the Air element within you.

If the Element of Air is aspected, check you are able to be detached, think clearly and communicate precisely. Ensure you are valuing emotion and intellect equally, that your ideas are practical and goals realistic. You may be vulnerable to the thoughts of others, becoming easily confused or bored.

This element is associated with the Solar Plexus and Heart Chakras and the Animal and Human Realms, and it is linked to lungs and the nervous system. Imbalances in this element may show up as stress, mental imbalance, eccentricity, fanaticism and unreasonably rebelling against constraints. Crystals cast onto the Element of Air can help you develop discernment so that knowledge transmutes into wisdom.

If you need to develop the ability to think clearly, concentrate and discern, draw upon the Element of Air. At times when you need to express yourself with clarity, do several things at once or think especially quickly, let this element be your ally. If it is balanced and integrated within your energy system, you will have the wisdom to transcend pain and suffering to find spiritual truth and freedom from illusion.

To harness the healing qualities of Air you may find it helpful to use sound as a healing tool. Try chanting, listening to music or using instruments. It is important to express your thoughts and feelings; consider some form of counselling or write your ideas down in a reflective journal. Positive affirmations repeated regularly can also be useful. Utilize the breath to help relax the body and release old thought patterns. You may need to employ several different therapies to appeal to the versatility of the Element of Air.

THOUGHT • COMMUNICATION • IDEAS

The Element of Fire

The Element of Fire relates to the vital life force within your being. It is the dynamic part of you which fuels your enthusiasm, sexuality and creativity. With too much Fire energy 'burnout' can occur, whereas too little causes total depletion and lack of spark.

If the Element of Fire is aspected, look at your energy levels and try to introduce some moderation into your life. It is likely that you are living life to excess which can result in exhaustion or hyperactivity. You could find yourself tending to act without first thinking things through and this impulsiveness and haste could cause problems for you or those around you.

Fire is usually associated with the Human and Animal Realms and Heart and Solar Plexus Chakras, and is linked to the ability to feel devotional love for others. Crystals cast onto the Element of Fire can encourage you to combine the magical powers of creativity tempered with unconditional love in order to manifest the flame of spirit on Earth.

Utilize the Element of Fire if you need to cleanse from your soul old thoughts and patterns of behaviour – burn up doubts and fears. Be aware of and avoid a tendency to get bored easily, be impatient or quick tempered. When the Element of Fire is balanced, you can initiate wondrous projects, inspire others with your confidence and radiate love to all around you.

To harness the healing qualities of Fire seek creative pursuits which ignite your imagination and open your heart to the 'love ray'. Find some form of movement or exercise which helps burn off excess energy. Incorporate fire and smoke into your self-healing rituals, try smudging with herbs or incense, and lighting candles – firewalking may appeal to the more adventurous! Heat treatments such as saunas or steam baths may also be of use. You may need to travel to sunny climates at times or possibly use light and colour therapy.

VITALITY ● INSPIRATION ● CREATIVITY

The Element of Ether

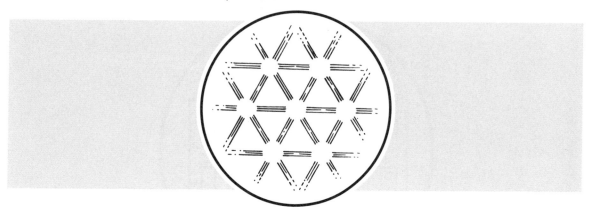

Ether is considered to be the source – the primary, formative force – from which the other four elements flow. Everything comes from and returns to Ether – it is the matrix upon which all physical forms are built. Ensure the Element of Ether is balanced within you when you need to strengthen your spiritual connection.

If the Element of Ether is aspected, you need to nourish and feed your soul and make time for spiritual pursuits. Re-establish your spiritual contacts and connections, and reflect on how you can make your life more whole in order to integrate the Divine with the physical.

Ether is associated with the Throat and Brow Chakras and the Planetary and Angelic Realms. It is the energetic band between celestial and physical realms. Crystals cast onto this element can help you learn how to live on Earth in accordance with spiritual law and universal principles.

Draw upon the healing rays of Ether when your celestial vibration is undergoing change, or you wish to synthesize the heavenly influences within your earthly vehicle. When your energy system is in a state of flux as you wait to form new vibrationary patterns, Ether holds the space and creates the void into which the new vibration may flow. Although unformed and less physically tangible than the other four elements, it is essential for your well-being, as it permeates your whole energy system. Ether holds the pattern of possibilities which your soul may act upon in this lifetime.

To harness the healing qualities of Ether, seek therapies which consider the soul more than the physical. Explore vibrational healing techniques such as sound, colour, gem and flower essences. Remember that the vibration of the therapist is more important than the therapy itself, so ensure your therapist is working at a soul level, with purity of purpose and a clear light-filled channel. Give yourself sufficient time and space to integrate the various strands of energy which are dancing through your life.

SOURCE ● INSPIRATION ● SYNTHESIS

The 'All That Is' Sphere

This sphere is unique in the Healing Wheel. It does not relate to a specific part of your energy system, but rather encompasses the entire system and every part of your being, including the elements, realms and chakras.

The 'All That Is' sphere is represented by the yantra and the Sanskrit 'om'. The yantra is a traditional meditation tool, similar to a mandala. It takes the meditator through all levels of consciousness from the most physical outer aspects into the most spiritual centre point. The om is known as the supreme syllable and is thought to symbolize eternal wholeness. It is the creative tone from which the world originates. (*For further information on meditation, see Using Crystals for Healing, page 104.*)

This sphere is most closely associated with the Crown Chakra, but its influence is even more widely felt and often indicates profound life changes. When a crystal aspects this sphere, its healing qualities should be absorbed at all levels of consciousness and within every facet of your being. Look at these qualities and learn what energetic changes and healing processes are taking place, and what significance they have for you. Focus on working with this crystal in as many different ways as possible. You could carry it around with you in your pocket; meditate with it; or place it under your pillow at night. However, it is sufficient to leave the crystal in place on the Healing Wheel or place it on the sphere printed here and absorb the healing frequencies throughout your whole being.

COMPLETION ● LIFE CHANGES ● ABSOLUTE ● UNIVERSAL

CRYSTAL INTERPRETATIONS

If a crystal falls in this sphere, try holding it and focusing on what this crystal really means to you. The following ideas are given for guidance only; more detailed information on each crystal is given in Chapter One (*see pages 14–25*).

AMETHYST
Amethyst suggests a theme of transformation and transmutation; allow profound changes to take place in many areas of your life.

AVENTURINE
Aventurine indicates a process of expansion; let your physical, mental, emotional and spiritual aspects stretch to embrace a broader spectrum of vibrations.

BLUE LACE AGATE
Blue Lace Agate conveys a theme of harmony and balance; look at ways of making your life more restful and calming.

CITRINE
Citrine brings a warming influence into your energy field; find ways of enriching your being with celestial wisdom.

CLEAR QUARTZ
Clear Quartz suggests a need for clarity and structure; look at how you can become more focused and follow a specific direction.

GOLD TIGER EYE
Gold Tiger Eye brings protection and strength; the energies around you have a more solid and practical vibration.

HEMATITE
Hematite suggests a theme of predestined events; you may consider surrendering to the inevitable.

RED JASPER
Red Jasper carries qualities of endurance and practicality; let your healing process manifest all the way through into the physical.

ROSE QUARTZ
Rose Quartz suggests that you look at ways of bringing reconciliation and unconditional love into your life; forgiveness can be one of the greatest healers.

SNOWFLAKE OBSIDIAN
Snowflake Obsidian illuminates even the darkest parts of the energy field; use this light wisely to see a way through.

SNOW QUARTZ
Snow Quartz implies a need for purification and cleansing; move on from old patterns into a new space and frequency.

UNAKITE
Unakite helps to unite seemingly conflicting aspects; accept the duality of nature and then let it blend within you in one harmonious whole.

Sample Reading

Jeremy is a writer. He tends to overwork at times and not give himself sufficient time and space for his own healing. He did not want a reading but a quick and effective healing.

CASTING ONTO THE HEALING WHEEL

He asks, 'What healing qualities do I need at this time?' While focusing on the question, he selects five crystals from the pouch: Citrine *(inspiration)*, Snow Quartz *(purification)*, Unakite *(unification)*, Rose Quartz *(reconciliation)* and Red Jasper *(manifestation)*. Then, casting the crystals onto the Healing Wheel, he asks 'Where do I need these healing qualities in my energy system at this time?' Citrine aspects the **Crown Chakra**; Snow Quartz aspects the **Heart Chakra**; Unakite aspects the **Plant Realm**; Rose Quartz aspects the **Animal Realm** and Red Jasper aspects the **Element of Fire.**

THE INTERPRETATION

The golden inspirational theme of **Citrine** is flooding into the whole energy system via the **Crown Chakra**. This can indicate a change in vibration which could account for the fatigue, which may be unavoidable due to the profound shift in consciousness taking place at this time.

Snow Quartz on the **Heart Chakra** shows a need to purify and cleanse. This chakra is a point of balance and a gateway through which he can access the spiritual vibrations. The cleaner and clearer this part of the energy system, the clearer the light will flow through.

Red Jasper aspecting the Element of Fire suggests that Jeremy needs to earth his inspirational spark in order to manifest his creative abilities and avoid burnout. He may need to take up some physical activity which creates a safety outlet for his excess energy. This seems to be an important key in his self-healing process, especially as the Heart Chakra and Element of Fire can echo similar themes within the Healing Wheel. Focusing on this aspect may lead to a realization of his deepest heart-felt dreams.

Rose Quartz in the **Animal Realm** is a reminder to respect and value his own instincts and primal needs. It is suggesting that through loving himself more and being gentle and kind he can find the courage to act in the appropriate manner to meet his own needs. He may also find that this will allow him to become calmer and more balanced, and less prone to angry outbursts when stressed.

Unakite in the **Plant Realm** suggests a need to balance and integrate, especially with regard to emotions. Jeremy might be able to derive great benefit at this time from healing therapies that involve plants; for example, he might wish to arrange for regular aromatherapy sessions, start taking herbal remedies or more simply ensure that he goes out walking in natural environments and consciously breathes in the life force radiated by the plants and trees.

Jeremy was asked simply to absorb the healing vibrations for a few moments.

SUMMARY

As two chakras, two realms and one element were aspected, this reading seems to indicate a complete shift in the whole energy field is taking place. This is especially reinforced by the fact that the Crown Chakra is aspected. A crystal

CRYSTAL CASTING

Jeremy asks: 'What healing qualities do I need at this time?'
He then selects five crystals.
Jeremy then asks: 'Where do I need these healing qualities in my energy system?'
He then casts the crystals onto the Healing Wheel.

Citrine aspecting the Crown Chakra indicates a profound shift in consciousness.

Red Jasper aspecting the Element of Fire indicates a need for earthing in order to manifest desires.

Snow Quartz aspecting the Heart Chakra shows a need to purify and cleanse.

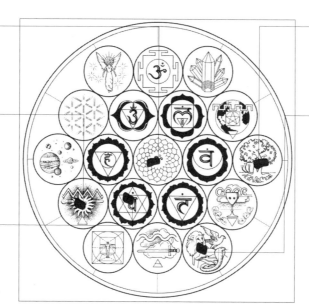

Unakite aspecting the Plant Realm suggests a need to balance and integrate the emotions.

Rose Quartz aspecting the Animal Realm suggests a need to value instincts and primal needs.

working on this chakra will usually indicate the theme of the healing – it also affects each sphere as it resonates throughout the whole energy system. The overall theme seems to be one of accepting and absorbing inspiration and learning to integrate this, even into physical daily life. This requires balance and a review of the various components required for a healthy lifestyle. For example, there may be a need to get more physical exercise, take particular care with diet and ensure that there is a greater degree of balance.

POSTSCRIPT

A few days later, Jeremy confessed that he had been feeling overworked and needed desperately to take time out but he seemed to be a victim of his own success, receiving more and more commissions. As a freelance writer his type of work is erratic and he feared refusing any offers. The healing helped him to get in touch with his own needs and he resolved to go back to practising Chinese martial arts and resumed his daily tai chi regime in the local park. To ensure that he was receiving healing on a more regular basis he had booked a series of aromatherapy sessions. He also felt that he should trust that the flow of inspiration would continue and he did not need to work all the time. In fact by being more balanced and healthier he would probably work more effectively and receive more inspiration – this would ultimately raise the quality if not the output of his work.

CHAPTER FIVE

Using Crystals for Healing

Crystal healing is the use of crystals and gems to promote balance and harmony at all levels within the energy system – physical, emotional, mental and spiritual. This balance brings about a healthy state of being.

How to incorporate crystals into healing

The following information only relates to healing with crystals using *The Crystal Wisdom Kit*, and specifically the Healing Wheel. There are many books on the subject of crystal healing *(see Bibliography and Further Reading, page 111)*; please refer to these if you would like to learn more about the subject generally.

If you feel you would like to develop your skills to become a professional practitioner, please find an appropriate training course. Ideally, look for one which gives you a recognized professional qualification, with membership to an association that has a code of conduct and a practitioner register. You should also ensure that you can gain insurance after you have completed the training. The contact address for the International College of Crystal Healing is given on page 112.

WHY USE CRYSTALS?

Crystals are tools which can help you focus when tuning into the healing vibration. There are many possible explanations for their healing powers. They contain patterns of perfection and symmetry within their crystalline structure – these patterns can then be emulated by the energy system. It is a little like the way a tuning fork may be used to give an example of the right note – a person finds it easier to sing in tune when guided by an experienced singer with perfect pitch. In the same way, crystals give us a template of perfection to aspire to.

HOW DOES IT WORK?

No healer or crystal heals anyone! The true healing process takes place within the person themselves. In other words, all healing is a form of self-healing. However, the crystals and the healer act as catalysts to activate this process. It is as if they act as a temporary scaffolding system to help 'jump start' the patient's own healing. The crystals can also act as points of focus, shaping the universal healing energy to make it more accessible to both patient and healer.

ATTUNEMENT

Additionally, crystals assist the attunement process which has three aspects:
  1. Earthing the healing vibration
  2. Linking to the healing vibration
  3. Ensuring the healing vibration flows freely and clearly.

EARTHING
Earthing, sometimes called 'grounding', is the process by which the human energy system connects to the planet. It is essential that both healer and patient be earthed to ensure that the healing process is carried out safely and effectively. The stronger the connection to the Earth, the higher the healing vibration that the healer can carry on behalf of the patient. By earthing the healing process, the healing vibrations will enter the whole energy system into the physical.

Crystals obviously come from the earth and some, in particular, have strong grounding potential. Discover which crystals in your kit help you to ground by holding individual crystals for a few moments and observing how you feel. If the crystal is helping you to ground, you may feel more clear-headed, physically slightly heavier, and sometimes you can even experience a tingling on the soles of the feet.

LINKING

Linking to the healing vibration might be described as the process you use to make a link to your source of spiritual inspiration. Some call this source the Divine Light or the Universal Life Force, and others simply refer to this energy as God. There are many different names; what is important is that you use words that feel right and true for you and that you are clear about the meaning they have for you.

Crystals have the ability to inspire. In the same way as a breathtaking view or a beautiful piece of music can uplift your spirits, so can certain crystals with their natural beauty and magic. Find which crystals lift your spirits when you hold them.

FLOWING

Now that the energy field is strongly grounded by being connected to the earth and a powerful link to the light has been established, it is vital that the Divine Light can travel through you clearly and freely. In healing terminology this would be called having a clear 'channel'.

It is quite usual though for there to be small interruptions in the flow, possibly caused by tension and stress in the body or blockages in the energy field. By holding certain crystals in your hands or on the body where the blockages seem to be, the energy is dispersed and channel cleared.

The above three-fold process is collectively referred to as the 'Attunement Process'.

Healing does not mean curing. In fact, healing is a somewhat misleading term. It is important to try to develop a detachment to results and outcomes of your healings. It is impossible to know the depth of the effect and it may not always register in an obvious physical way. Often the most powerful healings are also very subtle, but life changes can unfold in the months that follow. Do not underestimate the power of crystals and be prepared to expect the unexpected!

PERMISSION

This is one of the most difficult aspects for novice healers to accept. However, it is very important to consider the spiritual and ethical implications if you decide to send someone healing without first gaining their express permission.

Firstly, at a practical level, it is very helpful if the person participates in their own healing process. It can be very disempowering to be told later that you were sent healing. It could be considered invasive, however well intentioned your motives are.

Secondly, every being has a right to keep their illness or imbalance. As mentioned earlier in the Healing Wheel chapter (see page 71), it is often necessary to go into a state of imbalance to find a new level of equilibrium. Therefore illness and disease can be an essential part of the soul's spiritual evolution. A healer who decides to intervene by giving healing could actually be 'interfering'!

Thirdly, it is useful to reflect on why you wish to send someone healing – are you fulfiling a need within you, rather than unconditionally helping them?

On a practical note, it is usually considered acceptable under Universal Law for permission to be granted by the parent or guardian on behalf of a child, the owner of a pet and, in the case of someone in a coma or other serious illness, by the next of kin.

Please remember, the healer does not mentally decide which crystal should be used nor where it should be placed. The healer 'holds the sacred healing space', acting as a channel for Divine Light, while the patient makes their own choice regarding the crystals and their placement. It is very tempting to want to try to cure a condition by treating a particular area with a crystal that is reputed to have certain healing qualities. However, there is no way of knowing if this is the source of the problem and whether it is appropriate or not for that condition to be treated. For example, a patient may be suffering from a sore throat and you may feel you want to place a crystal on the Throat Chakra. However, when the crystals are cast, the Solar Plexus Chakra is aspected. This might indicate that the throat is being affected by a block in the Solar Plexus Chakra.

Also, it is far simpler, as well as much more effective, to use the casting method and let the Divine Light heal through you.

Note: *All the guidelines for healing given in this book relate only to the use of crystals as a part of this kit. If you follow the recommended procedures and variations, incorporating the step-by-step procedures, especially with regard to the attunement process, then you will work safely and effectively on yourself and others.*

EXERCISES TO FAMILIARIZE YOURSELF WITH CRYSTAL ENERGY

In addition to using your crystals for the various readings and healing techniques, you may wish to get to know your crystals better by working with them energetically and tuning in to them. Some ways of doing this are described below.

1. Hold one of the crystals in one hand then change it to the other hand and see if you can discern a difference, however small. Does it feel more comfortable, as if it belongs in one hand rather than the other?

2. Hold the crystal in one hand and hold the other hand, palm down, over it. Very slowly move your top hand closer to the crystal, then further away, reaching a distance of more than ½ metre (2 feet). You may be able to feel some sensation in one of your hands, possibly some heat, a tingling or a feeling of a slight breeze. Occasionally some people feel a magnetic pull towards or repulsion away from the crystal. Try this exercise with several of the crystals in your kit and note down the different responses.

3. Spread all twelve of your crystals on a flat surface in front of you, leaving at least a 10 centimetre (4 inch) gap between them. Then try to 'scan' the energies with one of your hands – gently pass your hand, palm down, over the crystals and note if you feel any sensations as you move over them. In this way you learn to register the resonance of the individual crystals in your kit. It may take some time at first, so please persevere. When you become confident with this, you can hold a question in your mind and use this method to select your crystals rather than drawing them out of the pouch.

MEDITATION

At various points in this book we refer to a need to meditate on certain aspects. Meditation is simply creating the right state of being, so you can listen to your inner being and Divine Guidance. Everyone has their own way of doing this and you do not need to follow a formal technique. Find what works for you!

First of all, find a time and place when you will not be interrupted. Have a point of focus – a candle flame can be ideal for this. Make sure you are comfortable. Sitting is often preferable to lying down as this helps avoid the usual pitfall of falling asleep!

It is usually helpful to relax the physical body. An effective and simple method of doing this is to stretch your arms upwards and to the side. Then take long, slow breaths. Try to breathe deep into your diaphragm – it is helpful to imagine that there is a balloon in the lower part of your stomach and you are trying to inflate this as you breathe in. When you breathe in do not pull your stomach in – but rather allow it to expand to accommodate the balloon! This type of diaphragm breathing just on its own can be very relaxing and stress-releasing.

Alternatively, use visualization to help you relax. For example, imagine that you are sitting in a place of great beauty and peace. Try to build the mental image using all your senses. If there are flowers in your special place, then see their colours, smell their fragrance and touch their petals. (See below for more detail on visualization.)

Once you are in a relaxed state, you can reflect on one of the symbols that may have been indicated in one of the wheels or hold a crystal and try to hear its message for you. By meditating in this way, you are becoming open and receptive to 'hear' finer vibrations.

VISUALIZATION

To visualize means simply to create an imaginary mental picture of a situation or event. Also known as imagery, visualization is a useful technique to aid the process of relaxation and healing. If you can imagine yourself being placed in a relaxing situation then your physical body can actually respond and you will feel more relaxed. For example, you may find it relaxing to imagine that you are resting in the calm and peaceful surroundings of a beautiful garden being bathed in warm sunlight. The more evocative the scene is for you then the more you will benefit from it and be able to relax.

Visualization does not just involve sight and not everyone visualizes in a 'seeing' way. Do not worry if you cannot 'see' anything as visualization can and does work in many different ways.

When creating a visualized image it is helpful to use all your senses. For example, if you are imagining yourself in a relaxing garden, you might find it helpful to imagine the wonderful array of fragrances and scents which emanate from the surrounding flowers and freshly mown grass. Really enjoy the sensation of smelling the flowers as you breathe in their various aromas. You might also wish to imagine the feeling of cooling grass beneath your feet and a soothing gentle breeze caressing your skin. Add to the picture the sounds of birds singing and running water from a distant brook or waterfall and you can complete your picture of a relaxed retreat and haven.

Remember to choose your own images. These will always be more powerful and effective for you than images chosen by someone else.

AFFIRMATIONS

It may seem a strange idea but making positive statements about how you wish to feel can bring about the desired change. If you 'affirm' that you are willing to be open to change and healing then the process will unfold much more easily and naturally. If you have low self-esteem and a negative self-image, it will help greatly to use affirmations such as 'I love myself' and 'I am a strong positive and healthy being'. In time these positive statements will replace the negative thoughts which have become ingrained into your thinking pattern – it is like letting go of old bad habits. Repeat your affirmations several times a day.

There are three key points to remember when you are working out a suitable affirmation for yourself. Keep the affirmation:

- Positive
- Present
- Personal.

Always use a positive statement such as, 'I am relaxed and happy'. If you use a statements such as, 'I am not stressed', the subconscious seems to obliterate the 'not' and you end up with a very different affirmation!

Keep your statement in the present tense – it does not work to say 'I am going to become relaxed' – you need to tell yourself how you are now in the present moment, then your body will follow suit. Using the future tense means you will never reach that state!

Avoid using the third person or collective such as 'one is relaxed' or 'we are relaxed'. Make the statement personal to you by using words such as 'I', 'me', 'mine'.

Some good affirmations could be:
I love and value myself
I am relaxed and happy
I feel safe and secure in the world
I am a beautiful and radiant being of light.

CLOSING DOWN

It is essential to always 'close down' your energy centres after healing, meditating and even giving a brief reading with one of the wheels. 'Closing down' means slowing the energetic frequencies in your system back down to a level where they can happily and safely operate at the more mundane earthly level.

When you tune in to give readings and heal-ings, meditate or do the energy sensing exercises mentioned here, you will inevitably open the chakras, which will consequently speed up with increased energy flow. A reverse process must be implemented.

As it is so very important, please always follow the guidelines set down in the relevant chapters for completing readings and healings.

Case Study

Anne is single, aged forty-one and lives in London. During the last three years she has undergone many changes which have brought about a spiritual evaluation of her whole life. The recent death of a dear friend had a profound effect on her. A close relationship is currently undergoing great change which is inevitable, but nonetheless disturbing. Aspects of her work life have been frustrating and most unsatisfactory as she has been forced to lower her standards to accommodate the wishes of others. She feels it is time to examine some of the fundamental spiritual principles by which she now wishes to lead her life. She has become increasingly disenchanted with her present lifestyle, and recent circumstances seem to be forcing her to look at what she really wants from life and what is important. She has recently qualified as a vibrational healer and her healing work involves using crystals and colour. At this stage, she does not feel ready to make healing her full-time occupation, so maintains her regular day job as a designer on a part-time basis, but does not find it wholly satisfying.

Anne comes requesting both a reading and healing. She feels quite uncertain and directionless at the time of the consultation. It is as if she is in a state of limbo waiting for something to happen, but is not quite sure what. Also, she is concerned that she should be 'doing' something, but does not know what it is. Having just completed a long and arduous healer training course she needs to know what her next step should be.

While her main reason for seeking the reading is to be given a sense of spiritual direction and clarity, Anne is also suffering from a sore and stiff neck and shoulder, probably, she feels, due to stress, anxiety and overwork. Also, various family members have been very demanding of late and she feels disloyal and inadequate when she is not able to give all that seems to be expected from her, resulting in feelings of frustration and at times even irritability which then turns into guilt.

THE LIFE WHEEL

To begin with Anne casts onto the Life Wheel to gain an understanding of the current and future trends surrounding her. Anne asks 'What influences are active in my life at this time?' and selects five crystals from the pouch. She selects Red Jasper (manifestation), Snow Quartz (purification), Unakite (unification), Gold Tiger Eye (protection) and Hematite (preordination). Concentrating hard, she then asks 'Where do I need to focus these influences?' and casts the crystals onto the Life Wheel. They indicate the following life areas and symbols: Hematite falls on the twelfth life area, Philosophy, on the Eagle; Red Jasper also falls on Philosophy, on the astro-logical symbol, Neptune; Gold Tiger Eye falls on the perimeter of the sixth life area, Health; Unakite spans the fifth and sixth life areas, Pleasure and Health, resting on both runes, Beorc and Sigel; Snow Quartz falls on the fourth life area, Home, on the Heraldic Shield.

THE INTERPRETATION
Hematite and Red Jasper suggest an overall theme of transcendence and an indication that Anne is on the brink of a huge cosmic adventure. Hematite advises that she learn to anchor the Light within her physical life. Red Jasper suggests that dreams can now become reality with just a

little practical help from her. Anne felt that if she could only identify her dream she could metaphorically fly off into a new realm of consciousness. She also felt that these placings both confirmed and encouraged her feelings of wanting to explore the spiritual dimension further. She found these crystals really uplifted her spirits.

Because **Gold Tiger Eye** is on the outer perimeter of the **Health** area, its influence may be felt less immediately or at a more subtle level. In view of the increased responsibilities and demands occurring due to family commitments, this crystal seems to be a timely warning not to expend too much energy and keep an eye on health issues. This message was further reiterated by **Unakite** which exactly spanned the **Pleasure** and **Health** life areas, resting on both the runes. The message of these two life areas combined is to find pleasure and joy whilst working in service to others. Anne felt that this refers to the fact that she has recently felt 'bogged down' by responsibilities and she responded very positively to the idea that she should try to spend equal amounts of time playing as well as working. It was interesting that these runes were indicated: *Beorc* symbolizes 'birth of life' and *Sigel* symbolizes vitality, health and regeneration – it seems from this reading that Anne is undergoing a profound change in her energy levels and a healing process is taking place. She felt that, together with the **Gold Tiger Eye** placement, this was a subtle warning or at least a timely reminder to take time for herself.

The placement of the **Snow Quartz** on the *Heraldic Shield* in the fourth life area continues the theme of family issues and seems to show the importance of family links for Anne. The sense of unity and ancestry gives her strength and support, but at the same time she felt she still needs her own space – hence the impor-

tance of her own home being clear and pure. She expressed a desire for a 'minimalist' lifestyle at home at present and was tempted to start clearing out belongings in a major way.

To summarize, Anne seems to be at a critical turning point in her life. It is a momentous time for her and probably very appropriate she should seek a reading at this juncture. The reading confirmed her feelings that great changes were taking place and reassured her that she was 'on track'. She felt greatly heartened to sense that she had earned this spiritual promotion by her past efforts. She also thought the family pressures and demands could be put into greater perspective. If she could allow more time and energy for herself she would ultimately have more to give out to others. She resolved to make her own good health a higher priority. Her apartment was also due for a clear-out!

LIFE CHALLENGE

Anne felt that as she was actively meditating and working on her spiritual development, she would like guidance regarding the Life Challenge she was currently addressing. She returns all five crystals to the pouch, re-attunes and selects just one crystal which she then casts onto the Wheel. She chooses **Hematite** which interestingly had appeared to be the most significant and focal stone of the Life Wheel reading. The Hematite lands on the fifth life area, **Pleasure**, indicating a life challenge which directs Anne to channel her creative life essence with absolute purity. Anne particularly resonated with phrases such as being 'a pure and clear agent' and 'do you know your truth?'

She wrote down the entire challenge and felt this would be a useful focal point for her meditations over the coming weeks.

Anne was reminded of the significance of the

Hematite landing on the *Eagle* flying free – perhaps her Life Challenge was linked to this in some way. That idea inspired her and further motivated her to work actively with it.

INSIGHT WHEEL
Question One

Anne then looked to the Insight Wheel for more specific guidance about her Life Challenge. Her question is, 'Please give me insight regarding my Life Challenge.' All the crystals are again returned to the pouch. She selects three stones – Snow Quartz *(purification)*, **Clear Quartz** *(clarification)* and **Rose Quartz** *(reconciliation)* – and casts them onto the Insight Wheel while focusing clearly on the question. Snow Quartz falls on 'Be true to yourself'; Clear Quartz falls on 'Look before you leap'; Rose Quartz falls on 'Let it go'.

THE INTERPRETATION

Anne felt that 'Be true to yourself' perfectly echoed the message of the Life Challenge and continued the theme of a need for purity in body, mind and spirit. She also remembered that Snow Quartz had fallen into the fourth life area

and the clear-out at home became even more imminent!

'Look before you leap' is interpreted as a need for some caution before taking any action. Perhaps Anne needs to be clear about where she is going and why before taking off on any spiritual journeys and not following the first direction that appeared. She should learn discernment.

'Let it go' suggests a need to let go of preconceived ideas and expectations for the outcome of any spiritual project.

To summarize, Anne received clear confirmation that the Life Challenge she had selected was the right one. However, she was being cautioned not to let her impatience urge her into inappropriate actions and in fact a certain detachment was advised to help her not to rush into things and take time to choose the right course.

Question Two

Anne then asks for some guidance regarding a more mundane matter which had been getting her down lately. She asks 'How can I cope better with current family responsibilities and pressures?' She selects **Rose Quartz** *(reconciliation)*, **Citrine** *(inspiration)* and **Red Jasper** *(manifestation)*. Rose Quartz falls on 'Consider patience'; Citrine falls on 'Follow your desires'; Red Jasper falls outside the wheel so is disregarded.

THE INTERPRETATION

'Consider patience' was felt to mean that patience needs to be shown to Anne herself as

well as the family members who were causing the stress. If a more gentle and loving energy is introduced into the rather fraught situation then it may resolve more amicably.

'Follow your desires' seems, again, to say that it is important that Anne consider herself and her own needs and wishes when making plans with her family.

To summarize, the overall message of this reading seems to be one of moderation, a reminder that Anne needs to find the middle path of being helpful and supportive, but not at the expense of her own feelings.

HEALING WHEEL

Anne then turned to the Healing Wheel to experience its powerful healing qualities. She asks 'What healing qualities do I need at this time?' and selects five crystals from the pouch: **Clear Quartz** *(clarification)*, **Blue Lace Agate** *(harmonization)*, **Red Jasper** *(manifestation)*, **Snowflake Obsidian** *(illumination)* and **Rose Quartz** *(reconciliation)*. Then, casting the crystals onto the Healing Wheel, she asks, 'Where do I need these healing qualities in my energy system at this time?' Clear Quartz and Blue Lace Agate both fall on the **Base Chakra**; Red Jasper on the **Heart Chakra**; Snowflake Obsidian is positioned on the **Throat Chakra**; Rose Quartz spans the **Throat** and **Brow Chakras**.

THE INTERPRETATION

The **Base Chakra** is the source of vital life force and relates to the more physical aspects of the energy system. It was felt that Anne needs to work on restoring her connection with the earth. The presence of **Blue Lace Agate** suggests a need for balance and calm. When it was mentioned that walks in the countryside may be helpful, she was reminded of how much she misses taking time for 'walks in nature' and resolved to start making time for this. The **Clear Quartz** also positioned on the **Base Chakra** reinforces the message of Blue Lace Agate, but also suggests that Anne be clearer about her desire and willingness to be earthed. It was felt that she needs to take charge of her healing process and give it direction. Clear Quartz could also suggest a need to review her health regime and look at ways of cleansing and dispersing blockages. It was reiterated that the Base Chakra ensures that the whole energy system stays in balance and harmony – this centre is obviously of importance for Anne at this time as two stones aspected this particular sphere.

The **Heart Chakra** is aspected by **Red Jasper**. This suggests that Anne's energy system is feeling over-stretched and under extreme pressure. It was gently suggested that there was a risk of depletion and that perhaps Anne was giving out more than she was receiving, resulting in her own energy reserves running low. The Red Jasper seemed to be giving stability and strength to a chakra which was temporarily weakened – its solid earthing qualities enhancing the fragile Heart Chakra. As Red Jasper had appeared on two other occasions in the reading, it was obviously a significant stone for Anne and she was advised to reflect on the possible meanings it could have for her.

Snowflake Obsidian aspects the **Throat Chakra**. Anne picked up on the words relating to this chakra: 'recognize spiritual truth and your part in the cosmic plan' and felt strongly that this linked in very appropriately with her Life Challenge. She felt very excited and positive as it seemed further confirmation that she is about to make a 'breakthrough', especially when learning that the Snowflake Obsidian is also associated with breaking out of and through a difficult phase. She was also fascinated when it was pointed out that if the Throat Chakra is out of balance or blocked in some way, then stiff necks and sore shoulders can manifest. She felt the Snowflake Obsidian was bringing light into what had previously been a dark and untouched part of her energy system, clearing out old emotional debris, preparing the way for a new beginning.

Rose Quartz was spanning the **Throat** and **Brow Chakras** and Anne had felt strongly impressed to leave it in this position, even though the other crystals she had happily centred in their spheres. These chakras carry themes of forgiveness and acceptance – the Rose Quartz helps to balance and bridge the two energy centres. This placement was interpreted as indicating a need for Anne to love and forgive herself in order to acknowledge and accept her own truth. By doing this she will not only be able to communicate her truth but will also be able to hold the vision of her soul path without compromising her integrity. She was reminded to value her uniqueness and special gifts and make time for her own healing process as well as supporting and helping others.

To summarize, it was interesting that all five crystals aspected parts of the chakra system. The chakras are the points of the energy system which monitor the amount of energy entering and leaving the energy field. They are often clear indicators of our energy levels. Anne had been experiencing feelings of stress, frustration and irritability – all of which could have been caused by severe depletion in her energy levels and imbalances caused by her over-worked energy system trying to cope. The theme of this healing seemed to be one of restoring energy levels and balancing out – a specific healing took place within the Throat Chakra area, which was being highlighted at the physical level with the symptoms of the stiff neck and sore shoulder.

SUMMARY

Anne came seeking spiritual direction and clarity. From the very beginning of the session the crystals and symbols seemed to confirm that she was at a critical turning point in her life. This served to reassure her to trust her own intuition and relax more into the process. This was further reiterated by the guidance she received from the Insight Wheel to 'Let it go'. Her second question addressed to the Insight Wheel also indicated a need for moderation and patience. Work with the Healing Wheel indicated a need to restore energy levels and bring about a state of balance. The overall theme might be a reminder to let events unfold and take their course – spend less time 'doing' and more time 'being'.

POSTSCRIPT

A few weeks later Anne reported back on her reading. She felt she had been brought 'back on track' and had clarified many of her ideas. The reading had also served to focus her mind on a new project but wisely she had not yet taken action and was considering the various options, although a research project overseas was on the cards. She had also found the confidence and strength to answer back to more demanding family members and friends, putting her own needs and wishes higher up on the list. Her sore neck had cleared up almost immediately, but the shoulder had remained stiff and sore for a few days. She felt that the reading had 'made real' some very nebulous spiritual concepts and helped her to integrate her spiritual truth into her daily life. She felt her enthusiasm had been fired up and her energy levels were more buoyant and resiliant.

> Note: *It was interesting to see that Red Jasper and Rose Quartz were each picked three times. When a stone continually reappears in a reading it can be helpful to focus on its placement, either giving that part of the reading greater emphasis or using it as a starting point.*

Bibliography and Further Reading

Arroyo, S. *Astrology, Psychology and the Four Elements*. Nevada: CRCS Publication, 1975

Bailey, Alice. *Esoteric Astrology*. London: Lucis Publishing Co, 1989

Bauer, Dr Jaroslav. *A Field Guide in Colour to Minerals, Rocks & Precious Stones*. Edison, NJ: Book Sales Inc., 1992.

Bauer, Dr Max. *Precious Stones*. Boston: Charles E Tuttle Co., Inc., 1982

Becker, U. ed. *The Element Encyclopedia of Symbols*. Rockport, MA: Element, 1994

Blum, Ralph. *The Book of Runes*. New York: St. Martin's Press, 1993

Cirlot, J. E. *A Dictionary of Symbols*. London: Routledge, 1993

Clark, Anthony and Boyce, Stephen. *The Aquarian Rune Cards*. London: The Aquarian Press, 1993

Cooper, J. C. *An Illustrated Encyclopaedia of Traditional Symbols*. New York: Thames & Hudson, 1992

Cowens, Deborah and Monte, Tom. *A Gift for Healing*. New York: Crown Publishing Group, 1996

Eberhard, Wolfram. *A Dictionary of Chinese Symbols*. New York: Routledge & Kegan Paul, 1988

Fontana, David. *The Secret Language of Symbols: A Visual Key to Symbols and Their Meanings*. San Francisco: Chronicle Books, 1994

Frutiger, Adrian. *Signs and Symbols*. London: Studio Editions Ltd, 1991

Gerber. *Vibrational Medicine*. Santa Fe: Bear & Company, 1988

Hall, James. *Illustrated Dictionary of Symbols in Eastern & Western Art*. New York: Harper Collins, 1996

Hodgson, Joan. *Astrology – The Sacred Science*. Hampshire: White Eagle Publishing Trust, 1978

Holbeche, Soozi. *The Power of Gems and Crystals*. London: Piatkus, 1995

Judith, Anodea. *Wheels of Life*. Minnesota: Llewellyn Publications, 1993

Jung, Carl. *Man and his Symbols*. New York: Doubleday, 1969

Kozminsky, Isidore. *The Magic & Science of Jewels & Stones, Vols 1 and 2*. California: Cassandra Press, 1988

Kunz, George Frederick. *The Curious Lore of Precious Stones*. New York: Dover Publications, Inc., 1971

Lionel, F. *The Magic Tarot*. London: Routledge & Kegan Paul, 1982

Matthews, J. ed. *The World Atlas of Divination*. London: Headline Book Publishing, 1994

Meadows, Kenneth. *Earth Medicine*. Rockport MA: Element, 1989

Phillips, Clare. *Jewelery from Antiquity to the Present*. New York: Thames & Hudson, 1996

Rudhyar, Dane. *The Astrological Houses*. New York: Doubleday, 1972

Sasportas. *The Twelve Houses: An Introduction to the Houses in Astrological Interpretation*. San Bernardino, CA: Borgo Press, 1988

Tansley, David V. *Radionics & the Subtle Anatomy of Man*. Saffron Waldon, Essex: C W Daniels Co Ltd, 1972

Todeschi, Kevin. *The Encyclopeadia of Symbolism*. New York: The Berkley Publishing Group, 1995

Walker, Barbara. *The Woman's Dictionary of Symbols and Sacred Objects*. New York: Harper & Row, 1988

Wilson, Annie and Bek, Lilla. *What Colour are You?* Wellingborough, Northants: Turnstone Press Ltd, 1981

The Authors

STEPHANIE HARRISON

As Principal of the International College of Crystal Healing (ICCH), Stephanie travels extensively training healers and giving seminars and workshops on various aspects of healing. She has appeared on television, radio and in the press discussing the merits of crystal healing.

She has worked for many years in the complementary medicine field and lectures on a variety of esoteric subjects, including tarot, astrology, colour and sound healing, as well as her speciality subject, the use of crystals and stones for healing and meditation.

Stephanie is a fully accredited gemmologist, she holds a Certificate of Education and is a qualified NVQ assessor. She was actively involved in setting the UK National Training Standards for crystal therapists. In addition to her work as Principal of the ICCH, she now facilitates a specialist teacher training course for those who wish to teach within the field of complementary medicine.

She is constantly reviewing and exploring new applications and the development of traditional vibrational healing systems. Her work combining astrology and crystals is considered unique.

BARBARA KLEINER

Formally trained as a photographer, Barbara has travelled the world, specializing in expedition and travel photography. Her photographs have been exhibited at the Royal Geographic Society and have appeared in a number of publications. Her most recent assignment took her to Inner Mongolia with a TV camera crew making a documentary for an international knitwear manufacturer.

She also ran her own greetings card company, which for many years was renowned for its innovative designs and top-quality end products. Her cards were distributed internationally with outlets in the UK, Europe and the USA.

Barbara's esoteric training has included working extensively with Stephanie Harrison and other leading esoteric teachers. She co-facilitates tarot courses, crystal healing workshops and spiritual development classes. She has trained with the ICCH and offers healing and tarot consultations to clients in London. Her interests include the tarot, the use of symbols for healing and, in her spare time, she loves to travel.

Resources

CRYSTAL WISDOM WORKSHOPS

Deepen your understanding of the fundamental esoteric principles which underlie the concept of Crystal Wisdom. During the workshops Barbara and Stephanie will guide you through a series of exercises to enable you to experience profoundly the properties of the crystals and symbols and thereby strengthen the spiritual process initiated by Crystal Wisdom. You will be encouraged to explore ways of expanding and adding to the various divination and healing techniques already described, as well as discovering additional applications for your *Crystal Wisdom Kit*.

THE INTERNATIONAL COLLEGE OF CRYSTAL HEALING

Stephanie Harrison is the Principal and Founder of the ICCH, which operates internationally offering a formal healer training programme for those who wish to become professional crystal therapists. The training course takes place part-time over a minimum period of two years. The full and comprehensive syllabus incorporates the use of many different crystals and numerous crystal healing techniques.

The ICCH also offers introductory training days for those who wish to learn how to utilize the healing properties of crystals for themselves, their friends and their family.

If you would like to receive more information about training courses with Stephanie, Barbara and the ICCH please send a stamped self-addressed envelope to:
ICCH Head Office, 46 Lower Green Road,
Esher, Surrey, KT10 8HD, UK
Fax. 0181 398 4237

EXPAND YOUR CRYSTAL WISDOM KIT

Upon familiarizing yourself with your kit, you may wish to open up a world of possibilities by adding a new selection of stones to the ones you already have. Broaden your range of readings and discover many different ways Crystal Wisdom can be applied for divination and healing.

To receive a set of seven specially selected tumble-stones and instructions on their use, please order from:
Everlasting Gems, P.O. Box 10698,
Putney, London SW15 1ZD, UK

Orders in:
UK and Channel Isles: £4.75
Europe and Scandinavia: £5.25
Rest of the Word: £5.75

Please send payment by way of UK cheque, Eurocheque or International Money Order made payable to: 'Everlasting Gems'. The above prices include postage and packing.

Acknowledgements

AUTHORS' ACKNOWLEDGEMENTS

We would like to acknowledge everyone who has helped us during the exciting and creative journey of turning Crystal Wisdom into a reality.

We are especially grateful to the Angelic for their limitless patience, inspiration and guidance. We offer our heartfelt thanks to the Crystal Realm, without the infinite wisdom and radiant beauty of the crystals, this kit would not have been possible.

We are also indebted to our editor Zoë Hughes for her total confidence in this project and her continuous support and encouragement.

EDDISON•SADD EDITIONS

Commissioning Editor   Zoë Hughes

Copy editor   Sophie Bevan

Proof-reader   Michele Turney

Art Director   Elaine Partington

Design   Rachel Kirkland and Shefton Somersall-Weekes

Illustrators   Andrew Farmer and Anthony Duke

Production   Hazel Kirkman and Charles James